God's Hand
On My Shoulder

From WWII Bomber Pilot to Building Churches in Mexico

Joe Carl Martin, Jr.

with J.E. Martin

Original Book Cover Photo (2017)

7 April 1945: Pilot, 1st Lt. Joe Carl Martin, Jr., standing on the damaged tail section of his B-17G Bomber known as *E-Z Goin'* that was rammed by a German ME-109 during Martin's 25th Combat Mission

God's Hand On My Shoulder

From WWII Bomber Pilot to Building Churches in Mexico
Memoirs of Joe Carl Martin, Jr.
As told to and written with the assistance of J.E. Martin

Front Cover Photo Credit:
https://100thbg.com/ (Photo Gallery)

Back Cover DFC Photo Credit:
https://www.dfcsociety.org/

Except where noted, Biblical Quotations:
New American Standard Bible

Published by:
J.E. Martin
https://www.jemartinauthor.com/
Stories of Faith, Hope & Love

ISBN: 978-0-9993595-5-6

Library of Congress Control Number: 2017913363

For My Family

And we know that God causes all things to work together for good to those who love God, to those who are called according to His purpose.

~ Romans 8:28

Table Of Contents

ACKNOWLEDGEMENTS

By Joe Carl Martin, Jr.

The first person I have to thank is God Almighty. He is the reason I've lived as long as I have.

The second person I have to thank is my wife Virginia, who encouraged me to write down my memories. So, that's what I did in 2013 on my home computer. As I began to type, I mostly did bullet points of major events in my life. I also typed up a list of birth and death dates of family members. Then I started a new page that included more details, beginning with my father. And the memories just flowed. By the time I'd finished, I had 30 pages.

However, it wasn't until 2016 during a visit with my younger son Jerry and his wife Janice that Virginia asked Janice, a published freelance writer and copy editor, if she would write my story. I brought out my typed memories for Janice to look over. She then asked if I had any photos she could use in the book. Virginia gave her the two United States Air Force albums that my elder son Joe's wife Suzanne had assembled and presented to me on my 80th birthday. One album contains photos and memorabilia from my war years, and the other one holds my childhood and family memories. Suzanne later assembled a third album of the leftovers that would not fit in the other two. We gave this third album to Janice as well for use in this book. In addition, I loaned Janice one of the books from my personal library—*Flying Fortress: The Illustrated Biography of the B-17s and the Men Who Flew Them* by Edward Jablonski.

As Janice began to write this book, she did quite a bit of research in order to confirm the information that I had provided. From her own personal library, she re-read:

- *Piloto: Migrant Worker to Jet Pilot* by Lt. Col. Henry Cervantes, USAF (Ret., Strategic Air Command) and my former copilot.
- *Century Bombers: The Story of the Bloody Hundredth* by Richard Le Strange (Assisted by James R. Brown). The front cover of this book displays the same photo that's on the front of my [2017] book—the damaged tail section of the B-17G I flew during WWII. [The front cover was replaced with a different photo in this 2022 revised book. JEM]
- *Masters of the Air: America's Bomber Boys Who Fought The Air War Against Nazi Germany* by Donald L. Miller
- *Night* by Elie Wiesel (A first-person account of Eliezer "Elie" Wiesel of what occurred to him and his father as Jewish prisoners in Auschwitz and then Büchenwald concentration camps from May 1944 until April 11, 1945, when Büchenwald—near Weimer, Germany—was liberated by the U.S. Third Army.)

Janice also utilized the photographs and information found on the Official Website of the 100th Bomb Group (Heavy) Foundation (*https://100thbg.com/*), of which I am a member. She has detailed all the resources she used in the Bibliography at the end of this book. Various family members have provided additional photographs and information.

To everyone, particularly Janice, who contributed to and made this book possible—the story of my life—you have my profound gratitude and thanks.

Joe C Martin Jr

Joe Carl Martin, Jr.

ACKNOWLEDGEMENTS

By J.E. Martin

It has been my privilege to know Joe Carl Martin, Jr., as my father-in-law for the last fifty plus years. While working with Carl on his book, *God's Hand On My Shoulder: From WWII Bomber Pilot to Building Churches in Mexico,* I have come to learn many things about him that I didn't know.

Chief among the things his family has learned about Carl in recent years is that he was awarded the Distinguished Flying Cross for meritorious service during World War II. We would not have known this fact had it not been for Carl's wife Virginia. Shortly after they were married in 1997, Virginia found an unmarked cardboard box in the attic of the home Carl had shared with his first wife Evelyn, to whom he'd been married for almost 52 years, until her death from ovarian cancer in 1994.

The box contained a treasure trove of saved memories from Carl's childhood and his time in the United States Army Air Corps. Among the items Virginia found were Carl's First Lieutenant Bars, Pilot Wings, Army Dog Tags, Distinguished Service Medal, Air Medal, European-African-Middle Eastern Campaign (EAME) Theater Ribbon, American Theater Ribbon, Victory Medal, and his Distinguished Flying Cross.

In answer to Virginia's questions about the medals, Carl said that when the war ended, he gave his medals to Evelyn, and she put everything into the box that contained keepsakes his mother had saved from his childhood. And he never gave it another thought. Carl said the world was in the midst of returning to a peacetime life, and the men returning home from the war were told to get back to work. So, he did, finding a part-time job and returning to college on the new GI bill to finish getting his engineering degree that the war had interrupted.

As long as I've known Carl, he's never been a man who can just sit around and watch television. He's always kept himself busy doing something, whether working to support his family or tinkering at his workbench or attending church. Worshipping the Lord and caring for his family are two things that have always been important to Carl.

Unless you ask Carl questions about his life, he doesn't volunteer or boast about the things he's done, like serving his country as a bomber pilot during World War II or, after the war, building churches in Mexico. He also served on the board of the Harris County (Texas) Emergency Corps and became a certified EMT at an age when most people have settled into the retirement phase of their lives.

But, now, in this next phase of his life, Carl has taken time to write his story with Virginia's encouragement, and it is my privilege to help him do so. As we began this process, I interviewed Carl at various times to clarify and expand on his personal notes. I also utilized the assistance of published author PF Karlin who provided constructive critiques. My sister Judith A. Carpenter provided her editorial expertise. Her attention to detail and her patience were indispensable and most appreciated.

As you read this book, you will discover that Joe Carl Martin, Jr., has been known by different names. As a child, because he was named after his father, he was called Junior. In fact, his two nieces call him Uncle Junior. The rest of his family members know him as Dad or Carl or Pawpaw. To his crewmembers during the war, he was known as Joe or Lieutenant.

Thank you, Carl, for my freedom and for sharing your story.

Janice
J.E. Martin

Chapter 1

We do not remember days, we remember moments. ~ Cesare Pavese

The Beginning (1899-1928)

Cotton and Oil

All stories have a beginning, and this is mine, starting with my father and the Texas Oil Boom.

The discovery of oil at Spindletop on January 10, 1901, marked the beginning of a new era when men traveled on wheels powered by liquid fuel, and it spawned one of the largest petrochemical complexes in the world in the area around Beaumont, Texas.

The Lucas gusher at Spindletop, January 10, 1901. This was the first major gusher of the Texas Oil Boom.
~ https://en.wikipedia.org/wiki/Spindletop
~ https://www.lamar.edu/spindletop-gladys-city/index.html

In 1917, this discovery brought my father, Joe Carl Martin, Sr., (born in 1899) from Shongaloo, Louisiana, to Orangefield, Texas. He was 18 and went to work on a crew laying a pipeline through that part of the country, which was in the middle of the oil-drilling boom near Beaumont. They were hiring everyone who would work twelve-hour shifts, making five dollars an hour, while others were lucky to make ninety dollars a month.

Joe Carl Martin, Sr.

Shongaloo (pronounced Shawn-ga-lew) is an Indian term meaning "Running Water" or "Cypress Tree." Considered a village, Shongaloo has a total area of 7.9 square miles and is located in Webster Parish, Louisiana, approximately 55 miles northeast of Shreveport.

~ https://en.wikipedia.org/wiki/Shongaloo,_Louisiana

Dad and Mother's folks made a living in the logging industry as well as farming, particularly cotton.

Dad was from a family of five boys and six girls. He only had an eighth-grade education, because they all had to work in the cotton fields. Dad hated picking cotton, but times were tough. He had no other choice.

Mother's family is a little mixed up. Her father—my maternal grandfather—was Gordon Mallory, a railroad engineer who operated a steam engine, hauling logs out of the forest. He was married to Elenora Pinchard—my maternal grandmother—and they had three boys and two girls, one of whom would later become my mother, Cleo Mallory, who was born in 1904. Early one morning, the train's boiler blew up, killing Gordon.

Then Grandmother Mallory—Elenora Pinchard Mallory—married Clyde J. Martin (one of Dad's younger brothers), and they had four girls.

Joe Carl Martin, Sr.'s parents and siblings:
Top Row: Lummie; Clyde; Joe Carl, Sr.; Lillie; Lonnie
2nd Row: Dora; Addie May; Lizzie; Lula
3rd Row: Walter; Andrew Jackson Martin; Martha Jane (Amerson) Martin; Pearl

When Dinosaurs Roamed the Earth

Though the oil boom surrounding Spindletop had largely subsided by the beginning of World War I, its impact would last much longer. The abundance of oil found in Texas would fuel the expansion of the shipping and railroad industries, as well as the development of innovations such as automobiles and airplanes.

So, in 1917, when Dad heard about the pipeline being laid from Shreveport, Louisiana, to Texas, he struck out on his own. He ended up in the small town of Orangefield located half way between Beaumont and Orange, Texas. He went to work for an oil company by the name of Prairie Oil and Gas and soon became a driller. In those days, the day driller was in charge of the operation, same as a tool pusher is today. Dad was drawing good pay, so he sent money home to his folks. He also bought groceries for people in need.

By this time, America had entered World War I, and it fell to the oil and gas industry to increase its supply of fuel for merchant and military ships as well as keep up with the ever-expanding automobile industry. As an oil driller, Dad had one of those needed jobs on the Home Front, exempting him from military service.

Prairie Oil and Gas was sold to Sinclair Oil and Gas Company in 1932. The asset purchase of Prairie gave Sinclair the largest pipeline system in America. Expanding Sinclair Oil & Gas was a gamble for Harry Sinclair because the world was in the middle of the Great Depression.

Mr. Sinclair saved a number of petroleum companies from receivership or bankruptcy, and he acquired others to expand his company's operations.

Dad worked for Prairie/Sinclair Oil & Gas for 28 years.

Advertising writers first introduced Sinclair's famous green Dino in 1930 to promote Wellsville-refined lubricant—derived from Pennsylvania grade crudes laid down during the Mesozoic Era, when dinosaurs roamed the earth.

The campaign, featuring a dozen different dinosaurs, was a great success. In particular, the gentle but massive Apatosaurus became so popular that Sinclair registered him as a trademark in 1932.

~ https://www.sinclairoil.com/history/1930.html

The Honey Wagon

In 1920, Dad took a train back to Shongaloo to marry his girlfriend, Cleo Mallory, and they made their home in Orangefield in a company house provided by Sinclair. That's where I was born on September 1, 1923, at home with the help of a midwife. The closest doctor was nine miles away in Orange, but I must have turned out all right. I'm still percolating as I write down my recollections here in the year of our Lord 2013.

While living in Orangefield, we resided in four different company houses. The last one we lived in was moved about a quarter of a mile near a low water drainage ditch to a new location on company-owned land.

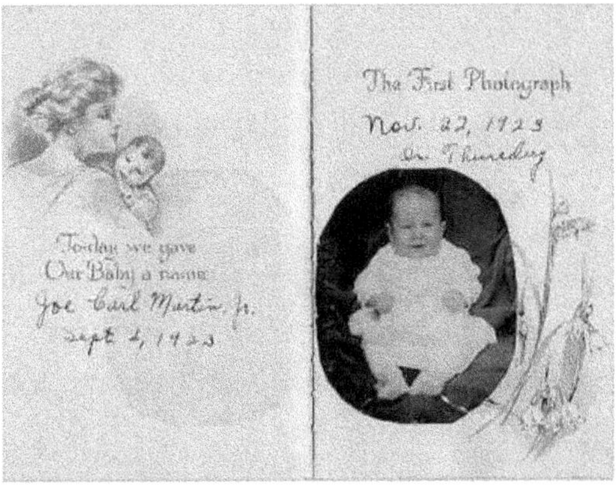

From Joe Carl Martin, Jr.'s Baby Book

To move the house, it was laid on large boards that were rolled on long pipes and pulled by a winch with large handles cranked by hand to pull the house forward. It took two days to inch the house along to its new location. The company only moved two homes to that piece of property, ours being one of them. The other house was occupied by a company superintendent.

The two houses sat on a high place across from a drainage ditch, and the company built a board road across the ditch to the main road so we could get out when it rained hard.

Cleo & Joe Carl, Jr.

It was the first time we had an indoor toilet. All of our previous homes had an outhouse a few yards from the back door. A man would come by with a wagon (called a honey wagon) and clean out the outhouse toilet once a week.

The company also built us a garage about 100 feet from the house for the company car Dad drove, and then they put a red picket fence around both houses.

On our section of the property (about one acre), Dad plowed and seeded a large garden and built a chicken coop for the chickens and a feed barn for the cows. We did a lot of home canning, which allowed us to give what we didn't need to friends and neighbors in need. Dad bought a push mower to mow the yard. When I got tall enough, I took over doing all the mowing.

Since we didn't have a hot water heater, Dad built a small building outside at the back of the house and put a shower in it with coiled two-inch pipe on the outside of the building so the sun could heat the water. For everything else, we heated water in a large washtub over an open fire in the backyard.

It wasn't a bad life. Some days were better than others.

I don't remember wanting something I didn't need. I just accepted my life as it was because I didn't realize there was any other life outside of where we lived.

Of course, I didn't realize that times were about to get a whole lot tougher.

Joe Carl, Jr., on the running board of the company car

Chapter 2

Doing all the little tricky things it takes to grow up, step by step, into an anxious and unsettling world. ~ Sylvia Plath

Growing Up (1929-1939)

Texas' Record Snowstorm of 1929

In 1929, I started first grade at the age of six and was held over for another year, but it was good for me. My teacher was also my Sunday school teacher in the local church. She invited the class to join her each Sunday, which I did. I had to walk about half a mile from home and hardly ever missed. I continued to walk to church until the summer of 1939. Then Dad was transferred to the Fairbanks Oilfield just outside of Houston's city limits.

Tomalene & Joe Carl, Jr.

Even though Dad didn't go to church because he was working all the time, he always sent me. He was a God-fearing man with good work ethics and a kind soul, and I never saw him drunk.

My sister, Tomalene, was born three years after me, on August 24, 1926. After her birth, Mother was crippled with the worst kind of arthritis. It left her bent over about 60 degrees and hardly able to care for herself, let alone us kids. There was no medical help for arthritis in those days, so Dad took Mother to Hot Springs, Arkansas, and Marlin, Texas, to take hot mineral baths and treatments.

Native American tribes called the location of Hot Springs [Arkansas] the "Valley of Vapors" and believed that the naturally hot springs had healing powers. Between 1892 and 1923, eight bathhouses were built on what's known today as Bathhouse Row.

Also in 1892, hot mineral water was found in Marlin [Texas] during the search for an artesian well. Dr. J. W. Cook promoted Marlin as a health center.

In 1925, Dr. Frank H. Shaw built a crippled children's clinic, providing treatment and therapy for handicapped children, including victims of polio and arthritis. He utilized the hot mineral water in a swimming pool and provided other muscle building therapy. The hospital was closed after World War II.

~ https://www.hotsprings.org/pages/history/
~ https://marlintx.net/about/

Joe Carl, Sr. & Cleo in Marlin, TX

We lived in Marlin one time for three months while Mother got her arthritis treatments. I went to school there at that time.

When we returned to Orangefield, I told all of my friends that I had gone to school way up north. For me, it *was* way up north, and it was very cold there in the winter. They used steam radiators to heat the school, but I was never warm, unless I could stand next to the radiator.

Marlin is located about 240 miles northwest of Orangefield or about 30 miles east of Waco, where a historic snowstorm occurred December 20-21, 1929.

Snow began falling in western portions of North Texas during the afternoon hours of December 20. Lightning and thunder accompanied the snow throughout the following night. By daybreak on December 21, several inches of snow had fallen across Central Texas from Junction to Lampasas, northeastward to Palestine and Athens.

Clifton and Hillsboro had already accumulated 16 inches of snow by daylight that morning. The heavy snow continued through much of the day, before tapering off during the late afternoon and evening hours. By late evening on December 21, the snow was confined to East Texas.

The storm lasted barely 24 hours, but the snow totals were nothing short of extraordinary. A swath of snowfall in excess of 12 inches was two to three counties wide. Along the axis of maximum depth, totals exceeded 24 inches, on par with the heaviest snowfalls in Texas' history. Clifton recorded 24 inches of snow in just 24 hours. Nearby Hillsboro tallied 26 inches.

Where the snowfall was greatest, temperatures plummeted into the single digits. In Waco, where the 13-inch total remains a 24-hour record for the site, the mercury fell to 2 degrees Fahrenheit, one of the coldest temperatures ever recorded there.

Cow Bayou and Alligators

When we moved back to Orangefield, after Mother's treatments, she talked her younger sister into coming to live with us. Beverly Mallory, or as we called her Aunt Bell, was about 13 years old.

Aunt Bell helped Mother with the cooking and the cleaning, and she took care of us kids. She was just like another mother and lived with us until about 1942. She left to marry a man by the name of Frank McDougle. They had a son Frank II and a daughter Nina Bell.

Beverly Mallory known as Aunt Bell

Frank McDougle was a welder, building ships in Houston for the war effort during WWII. He died in 1960 at the age of 51. By the time of Frank's passing, Dad had purchased 24 gravesites at the Brookside Cemetery on US 59 North. That's where Frank was laid to rest. Aunt Bell lived to be 89 years old. When she passed, she joined Frank in our family burial plot.

I went to school in Orangefield through the ninth grade, playing football and running track. I played a trumpet (a hand-me-down that I still have) in the band, but we never played at our football games. So, I went to the Port Neches High School (now known as Port Neches Groves High School) with my music instructor to play with the Port Neches school band at their football games, except when our team played their team. Our music instructor covered three separate schools—Orange High School, Orangefield High School, and Port Neches High School, ranging from six to twenty-five miles apart.

Joe Carl, Jr., taking a dip to cool off

We didn't have a public swimming pool, so we swam in local ponds, the rice canals or in Cow Bayou that ran near the edge of town. Someone put a cable across the bayou with a slide on it so we could slide over and drop down into the water.

There were alligators in all of the bayous, but they never hurt anyone. The Cajun men hunted the alligators all the time for their hides. They hunted at night using a pirogue type boat, a shotgun, and a spot light. There was a boat dock about 150 yards from our home, so I saw a lot of dead alligators being unloaded from their boats on the way to school in the mornings.

It was a different time back then. The Great Depression lasted from 1929 to 1939, the harshest adversity faced by Americans since the Civil War. We lived off the land, growing our own vegetables, using everything, and wasting nothing. In those days, Dad did a lot of squirrel hunting. It meant we had meat to eat most days.

Frozen Duck, Anyone?

In 1936, Dad raffled off his shotgun and got enough money to buy new bicycles for me and my sister for Christmas that year. I was thirteen and toured the countryside on that bike. One time, I rode my bike nine miles to the new Rainbow Bridge spanning the Neches River near Port Arthur. It was known as the tallest bridge in Texas and wasn't yet open for cars to drive on, so I pushed my bike to the top and sped back down just for the thrill of it.

In 1939, when I turned sixteen, Dad gave me a .410 gauge shotgun. It was a single-shot, break-open breech shotgun with a 22-inch barrel. I hunted birds, squirrels, and rabbits. More meat for the table.

In the winter months, I hunted ducks. The day I shot my first duck, it fell into a salt-water pond in freezing weather. I took off my clothes and waded into the pond to get that duck. The water was so cold I think everything on my body turned blue, but I kept hunting after I put my clothes back on. And I never went into the water again to get another duck.

When Dad bought his first car—a used 1934 Dodge 4-door sedan (a new car cost about $700)—we drove to Shongaloo for a vacation. Dad's parents, four brothers, six sisters, and all their kids still lived there.

Radios were scarce at this time, and Dad's car had a radio. In the evenings, with the lightning bugs rising from the grass, everyone would sit around the car on quilts or kitchen chairs they'd brought from their homes and listen to the Grand Ole Opry until the battery died. After that first vacation, we drove to Shongaloo every year to visit Dad's relatives. They were the only vacations we took.

Chapter 3

And my God shall supply all your needs according to His riches in glory in Christ Jesus. ~ Philippians 4:19

Coming of Age (1939-1941)

Transferred to Fairbanks, Texas

In 1939, when I was sixteen, I had a girlfriend by the name of Juanita Lowe. Her parents owned the local IGA store that had a large gasoline service station. Unfortunately, our relationship didn't last long, because Sinclair transferred Dad to the Fairbanks Oil Field located northwest of Houston. This old oil and gas field is now known as Woodwind Lakes subdivision and is located off US 290 and Beltway 8 (Sam Houston Tollway), which encircles the City of Houston.

> *In early 1997, Paul Anderson often drove through Woodwind Lakes to watch his family's dream house being built. But his excitement fizzled when construction crews uncovered an oil well in the front yard. By overlaying historical aerial maps from the 1950s, the Railroad Commission discovered that nearly one-quarter of Woodwind Lakes—or 150 homes—was built atop a vast oil and gas field.*
>
> *Fairbanks Oil Field, active from 1938 through the early 1970s, comprised 3,000 acres and several hundred wells that produced 42 million barrels of oil, according to state records. Warren Petroleum Company, a division of Gulf Oil Corporation and later acquired by ChevronTexaco, Inc., ran the Fairbanks Gas Processing Plant and the Ayers Compressor Station from the mid-1940s to 1966 on a total of 18 acres now within Woodwind Lakes.*
>
> *~ https://www.houstonpress.com/news/woodwind-lakes-subdivision-built-on-oil-and-gas-field-turns-on-neighbor-who-pointed-out-the-contamination-6574095*

When we arrived at the Fairbanks Oil Field, Sinclair had built us a new house on a 600-acre oil lease. The land was a bald prairie—tall weedy grass and no trees except along the creek that was about 100 yards from the house. The company drilled five gas wells that my father supervised. We also had a deep water well that was jettisoned into a 500-barrel wood tank via natural gas and was piped into our home. The tank flowed over into a pond and was used to water the cows Dad later acquired. The pond was great for swimming, too.

The house had two screened-in porches—one across the front and the other across the back. There was a roll-up cover on the back porch so we could close it during bad weather. That was my room, which I shared with the gas refrigerator. I had the coolest room in the house, which was good during the hot summer months. This was before air conditioning was even heard of in this part of the country.

FAIRBANKS, TEXAS. Fairbanks is on U.S. Highway 290 and the Southern Pacific Railroad, inside the western city limit of Houston in central western Harris County. The town was established in 1893 and named for its founder, who bought 106 acres at a site previously called Gum Island by the Southern Pacific trainmen because of the gum trees growing between White Oak Bayou and Willow Creek.

Fairbanks has had a post office since 1895. In 1914, the community reported a population of 75, a general store-saloon, and a grocery store. The number of inhabitants dropped to 25 in the 1920s and 1930s but by 1940 rose to 800. In 1942, Fairbanks reported a population of 800 and 35 businesses in the vicinity. A decline to 350 people in the 1950s was followed by a period of rapid expansion.

In 1962, the community reported 1,050 people and 45 businesses. This report, however, came after Fairbanks was annexed by Houston in 1956 and reflects members in surrounding communities. In 1980 and 1990, the population was still reported as 1,050, although considerably more people lived in the surrounding area.

~ https://tshaonline.org/handbook/online/articles/hvf03

Our nearest neighbors were the Swankiees, a dairy farmer about a mile south of us. I believe some of the family still live on the home place, but the area around them is completely built up with homes and businesses right up to the fence line of where I used to live. The 600 acres is still vacant and grown up with trees. The house and well-drilling equipment are all gone now.

Rationing

In its heyday, the Fairbanks Oil Field wells produced a form of light crude that could be used in a car in place of gasoline. During World War II, gasoline was rationed from 1941 through 1945 and required ration stamps to purchase fuel.

Ask anyone who remembers life on the Home Front during WWII about their strongest memories and chances are they will tell you about rationing. The war caused shortages of all sorts of things: rubber, metal, clothing, etc. But it was the shortages of various types of food that impacted just about everyone on a daily basis.

Food was in short supply for a variety of reasons. Much of the processed and canned foods were reserved for shipping overseas to our military and for our Allies. Transportation of fresh foods was limited due to gasoline and tire rationing and the priority of transporting soldiers and war supplies instead of food. Imported foods, like coffee and sugar, were limited due to restrictions on importing.

Because of these shortages, the U.S. government's Office of Price Administration established a system of rationing that would more fairly distribute foods that were in short supply. Every American was issued a series of ration books during the war. The ration books contained removable stamps good for certain items, like sugar, meat, cooking oil, and canned goods.

A person couldn't buy a rationed item without also giving the grocer the right ration stamp. Once a person's stamps were used up for a month, that person couldn't buy any more of that type of food. This meant planning meals carefully, being creative with menus, and not wasting food. More than 8,000 ration boards across the country administered the program.

Dad used the light crude produced by the wells for his car and gave his gasoline stamps to his good friend, Daris Rohrer, who owned a service station on the old Hempstead Highway. Mr. Rohrer, a gentleman of German descent, gave the stamps to soldiers passing through so they could purchase gasoline. Mr. Rohrer was also a good mechanic and made many friends as he helped people along the highway. He and his wife had one son named George, and we were good friends until his death in 2003.

Joe Carl, Jr. & George

Big Inch Pipeline of World War II

Dad's job in the oil and gas industry was invaluable not only during World War I but also during World War II.

A government/oil industry partnership built two petroleum pipelines from Texas to the East Coast that proved vital during World War II. "Big Inch" carried oil from East Texas oilfields. "Little Big Inch" carried gasoline, heating oil, diesel oil, and kerosene.

Beginning in August 1942, War Emergency Pipelines, Inc., launched the longest petroleum pipeline construction project ever undertaken in the United States—two pipelines spanning 1,200 miles.

Conceived to supply wartime fuel demands—and in response to deadly [German] U-boat attacks on oil tankers along the eastern seaboard, the Caribbean, and in the Gulf of Mexico—the oil pipelines were extolled as "the most amazing governmental/oil industry cooperation ever achieved." The final weld on the "Big Inch" was made in July 1943, just 350 days after construction began.

"Besides, without the outstanding cooperation of the Petroleum Administration for War with the numerous oil companies of America, World War Two very likely would never have been won by the Allies either," Miller explained in a 2002 lecture at George Washington University, Washington, D.C.

U.S. oil became indispensable for laying runways, manufacturing of synthetic rubber for tires, creating lubricant for guns and machinery and the distilling into gasoline (particularly at 100-octane levels) for use in trucks, tanks, jeeps, and airplanes.

"Now, it cannot be stated too forcefully," Miller concluded, "American oil, which amounted in all to 6 billion barrels, out of a total of 7 billion barrels consumed by the Allies for the period of World War Two, brought victory! Without the prodigious delivery of oil from the U.S., this global war, quite frankly, could never have been won."

~ https://aoghs.org/petroleum-in-war/oil-pipelines-big-inch/

Livin' Off the Land and Makin' Do

Our Sinclair-built house on the Fairbanks oil lease had about two or three acres under fence, which was made from oilfield pipe and sucker rods from old oil wells. We made a garden using a push plow, hoes, and rakes. To get started, Dad hired a man to plow up the ground using a horse and a turning plow. We grew corn, sweet potatoes and white potatoes, beans of all kinds, tomatoes, onions, lettuce, squash, cabbage, carrots, cantaloupe, cucumber, and okra. Aunt Bell and Mother canned most everything each year.

When we first arrived in 1939, Dad and I dug up trees in the creek bottom and planted them around the house for shade. We built a wash shed on the side of the garage, and, since we had no electricity, Dad installed a gasoline engine on our electric washing machine, which had a ringer on it to squeeze the water out of the clothes. We had a clothesline strung between two trees to hang the wash on. No automatic washers and dryers in those days.

We traded the electric refrigerator we'd brought with us from Orangefield for a gas-operated one. We used gas-operated lights and had a battery-powered radio. The gaslights were a little hard to read by, so Dad purchased a gasoline-powered fancy lamp to set on the kitchen table for us kids to study by.

On the oil lease acreage not being drilled, Dad made a deal with the company to lease that section so he could raise a few cows he'd purchased from Mr. Swankiee. And I learned to milk cows every morning and every evening. Dad ended up with over 200 head of his own cattle. He had a brand made—CM with an arrow "shot through" the initials—to identify his cattle.

Since we had plenty of milk, we made our own butter, and, again, that was my job, most of the time. We had two types of churns, one with a crank that you turned and the other one used a paddle on the end of a round stick that you plunged up and down in a ceramic butter churn. We had a wooden mold that formed the churned cream into one-pound blocks of butter.

When we needed ice, I would go to one of the aboveground gas pipelines and chip off the ice that built up on the line. I could get a large dishpan full every other day.

Besides taking care of the cows, I had to feed the chickens. My other job was catching a chicken, killing it, and cleaning it for Sunday dinner.

We never purchased chicken or meat from the store. I hunted the near-by woods and fished the pond on weekends. If we needed anything from a store, we went on Saturdays because it was over ten miles to a big store, and it took most of the day to make the trip. We only had one car and no telephone.

All the roads around the Fairbanks oilfield were made of dirt and shell bits with oil sprayed on them to help hold them together. In bad weather with lots of rain, we couldn't get out. Sometimes, when we had to get out, we'd wrap oilfield rope around the car wheels to give them traction in the mud.

It was about two miles of dirt and shell from our house to Little York Road, which had a hard-packed surface. Little York led to a road that would later become known as Fairbanks North Houston, which led to Hempstead Road. That's where the post office was located, along with a feed store that had a few groceries, a service station, and the Fairbanks Baptist Church.

After we got settled in the Fairbanks house, I started attending the Fairbanks Baptist Church, driving me and Tomalene most Sundays when I wasn't helping Dad, and when Dad didn't need the car.

Pastor D.E. Sloan led the congregation, and it was from him that I learned about the saving grace of God through Jesus Christ as my Lord and Savior. Fairbanks Baptist Church was where I met my future wife, Evelyn Lee Crotwell. Her father was a deacon in the church, so I watched how I acted around him.

The Crotwells—Mary Ann Milburn and Robert E. Lee Crotwell, Sr., and their children, Evelyn Lee Crotwell and her younger brother, Robert E. Lee Crotwell, Jr.—lived on 34th Street near the Hempstead Highway. At that time, 34th was a shell road, and it didn't go very far.

Since the school bus wouldn't come out the dirt road to our house, Dad

made a deal with his friend Mr. Rohrer to let me ride with his son George to John R. Reagan High School in the Heights area of Houston, where I graduated on June 4, 1941. Evelyn also attended Reagan and graduated in June of 1942.

That summer of 1941, I went to work in the oilfield, building board roads to the well-drilling sites and looking forward to attending college in the fall. My incentive for a higher education grew stronger with each passing day, with the summer sun beating down on my head, sweat pouring into my eyes, the smell of oil and diesel coating the inside of my nose and mouth, and my aching muscles screaming for relief. There were days when I felt like fall would never come.

But, fall finally arrived, and with it, the bombing of Pearl Harbor, a U.S. Naval Base near Honolulu, Hawaii, by the Imperial Japanese Navy Air Service on December 7, 1941. The attack killed more than 2,400 U.S. service members and civilians.

The day after the attack, President Franklin D. Roosevelt asked Congress for a formal declaration of war against the Empire of Japan. Congress obliged his request less than an hour later. On December 11, 1941, Germany and Italy declared war on the United States. Congress issued a declaration of war against Germany and Italy later that same day.

John R. Reagan High School, "The Pennant, 1942" (yearbook)

"Among Uncle Sam's fighting forces, now scattered across the globe, are many boys who are products of Reagan High School—some whose brilliance and achievement as students are marked impressively on school records and indelibly in the memories of their friends, others whose success was less outstanding—all of them now united in their stand for their country and their ideals. To the ardent loyalty and heroic courage of such as these, America and the world today turn for reassurance of ultimate victory and peace. It is altogether proper, then, that this book should be dedicated to Ex-Reaganites in the Service."

Chapter 4

More than anything else the sensation is one of perfect peace mingled with an excitement that strains every nerve to the utmost, if you can conceive of such a combination. ~ Wilbur Wright

Learning to Fly (1942-1944)

Traveling in Style

That fall, as planned, I started going to the University of Houston, working toward a B.S. in Engineering. By November 1942, I was a sophomore, having acquired 34 semester hours of the 120 required for a degree, with classes in calculus, general chemistry, plane surveying, and electricity and magnetism. I was on course for a graduation date of June 1, 1945.

However, during my second year, a recruiter with the United States Army Air Corps (USAAC) came to the campus, inviting the male students to join the USAAC now, but we wouldn't need to report for duty until after we'd graduated with our respective degrees. He told us we could wait to be drafted into the infantry, or we could volunteer now and become pilots. The prospect of learning how to fly sounded exciting to an impressionable 19-year-old, and I could do it after I got my degree.

So, I signed on the dotted line, along with quite a few other guys. Three weeks later, to my surprise, I received orders to report for induction in the United States Army Air Corps. I was told to bring a small suitcase with a change of clothes and personal toiletries, just in case. There was no "just in case" about it—I was in the Army Air Corps. I was now part of something important. My country needed me.

Evelyn and I hadn't discussed getting married. We were just really getting to know each other while I went to college and worked a part-time job. She was working as a sales lady at Kaplan's Ben-Hur Department Store in the Heights. But, with my impending departure into the Army Air Corps,

I didn't know what was going to happen to me, so I asked her to marry me. And she said, "Yes."

We were married on Valentine's Day, February 14, 1943, in the Fairbanks Baptist Church by Pastor Sloan. I only had a week to report for induction, so we spent our short honeymoon in Galveston, about 60 miles southeast of Houston. My Uncle Orville was already serving in the Army, and he'd left his brand new, light blue, 1940 Chevrolet convertible with me, and I promised to take good care of it. My bride and I drove to Galveston in style.

The original downtown post office was housed in the U.S. Custom House until 1962. ~https://en.wikipedia.org/wiki/United_States_Customhouse_(Houston)

Induction Day

All the recruits met at the main post office in downtown Houston in the U.S. Custom House. While I was in high school, I'd worked two Christmas seasons there as a mail stacker, so I knew right where it was located.

Like all new recruits, we had to submit to a complete physical to make sure we were healthy enough to serve. Once that was determined, we received several kinds of inoculations to protect us against any diseases we might get exposed to. By the time I got all my required shots, both of my arms felt and looked like pincushions. I walked over to the nearest wall, leaned against it, slid down to the floor, and rested a while. I wasn't alone in my misery.

After we were sufficiently recovered and dressed, we were lined up and sworn into the United States Army Air Forces (USAAF). I was classified as an Air Cadet and would be part of the Cadet Class of 1944, the year I would receive my wings. I found out later that the rank of Air Cadet was considered lower than an Army Private.

Enlistment Oath

"I, (state name of enlistee), do solemnly swear (or affirm) that I will support and defend the Constitution of the United States against all enemies, foreign and domestic; that I will bear true faith and allegiance to the same; and that I will obey the orders of the President of the United States and the orders of the officers appointed over me, according to regulations and the Uniform Code of Military Justice. So help me God."

~ Title 10 of United States Code § 502

Sheppard Field ~ Basic Training

We were taken by bus to the Union Station a few blocks away and departed for training at Sheppard Field in Wichita Falls, about 141 miles northwest of Dallas. It was my first train ride, but it wouldn't be my last.

Houston's Union Station, 1913.
~ https://en.wikipedia.org/wiki/Union_Station_(Houston)

During World War II, the USAAF established numerous airfields in Texas for training pilots and aircrews of USAAF fighters and bombers. Sheppard Field was where I received my basic Army training to learn about military life—how to march, salute an officer, make my bed, and handle a weapon, among other things. My pay was $18.95 per month, and it was the only place I saw rain, snow, and a dust storm all at the same time.

Unfortunately, I spent my first week of basic training in isolation with mumps and chicken pox.

Texas Tech University ~ Pre-Flight Program

From there, I went to Texas Tech University in Lubbock for a six-month pre-flight program. We stayed in the men's dorms and went to school eight hours a day, except Sunday.

The pre-flight program at Texas Tech began after the military realized it didn't have the resources available to train all the young men who wanted to be pilots. The Army reached out to civilian contractors to do initial flight training through the Civilian Pilot Training Program. Two Lubbock instructors, Clent Breedlove and M.F. Dagley, took up the challenge.

The pre-flight faculty provided the in-class portion of the training, which was held in classrooms on the Texas Tech campus. The two civilian instructors then provided eight hours of in-flight training at Breedlove Airport on East 50th Street and Dagley Field near 34th Street and Quaker Avenue. The course of rigorous education, physical training, and flight training for the cadets was designed to weed out anyone not capable of being a military pilot.

The pre-flight students took classes in math, physics, history, English, civil aeronautics, meteorology, and first aid, and were kept segregated from all the other students while on campus. There were posts and chains set up all around West Hall and Sneed Hall with signs on them that read, "Posted: Military training site. No trespassing."

While at Texas Tech, we took a few flight lessons in single-engine piper cubs with civilian instructors. I still have the record of my hours in the different planes I flew. One experience I had was when the instructor let me fly and the carburetor froze up when I cut the throttle for a stall. The engine stopped running, and we landed in a farmer's cotton field where he was plowing. The farmer came over and helped us pull the plane to the end of the row, and we took off.

~ https://www.piper.com/blog/piper-cub-history/

My graduation class at Texas Tech University.

Texas Tech pre-flight instructor pilots, in dark uniforms, pose with some of the students in one of the sections of the 309th College Training Detachment (CTD), the official name of the Texas Tech pre-flight program.

My graduation class at Texas Tech University.
I'm in the third row, second from the right.

During World War II, the United States fought for its life. Unbeknownst to many, so did Texas Tech University. In 2015, the 70th anniversary of the end of World War II brought about the tale of how a generation's fighting spirit turned the tides for the university and how it paid homage to its defenders.

~ https://today.ttu.edu/posts/2015/08/wwii-saved-united-states-and-texas-tech.

Santa Ana Army Air Base ~ Distribution Point

After I completed my education at Texas Tech, I was sent to Santa Ana Army Air Base in California, where the cadets were distributed to different flight schools all over the United States.

We traveled by train. Some were regular passenger trains and some were converted boxcars fitted with army cots and utensils to cook with on a regular stove vented to the outside. We ate out of our mess kits. During one long trip on a regular passenger train with dining cars, I volunteered to be a waiter and received several dollars in tips.

Evelyn followed me, by bus or train, to nearly every base where I was stationed. The base would hire the wives to work in the officers' club, so Evelyn got a job at each base.

> *The Santa Ana Army Air Base (SAAAB) was under the jurisdiction of the West Coast Army Air Corps Training Command Center, located on West 8th Street in Santa Ana, California. The other two centers were Southeast Army Air Corps Training Center at Maxwell Field, Montgomery, Alabama, and Gulf Coast Army Air Corps Center at Randolph Field, San Antonio, Texas. The latter two centers were activated on July 8, 1940, while SAAAB was activated on February 15, 1942. On June 20, 1941, the Army Air Corps became the Army Air Forces.*
>
> *~ https://www.costamesahistory.org/learn/saaab.htm*

I was at Santa Ana for just a few weeks, waiting to find out where I was going next. During that time, I had to learn to swim a marked mile in the Pacific Ocean. We also had to hike about 50 miles in the mountains outside of San Diego. We slept in one-man pup tents and ate K rations, which were lightweight packaged rations of emergency foods developed for the U.S. armed forces in World War II.

Rankin Aeronautical Academy ~ Stearman Biplane

From there, I went to Rankin Aeronautical Academy in Tulare, California. At the train depot in Tulare, we were loaded onto buses that took us straight to the airfield. The moment we stepped off the bus, we watched a plane spiral toward the ground. It crashed in front of us in the middle of the field. A fireball erupted, and the explosion shook the ground beneath us.

A friend standing next to me immediately ran over to the building that housed the offices to resign from the flight program.

My friend couldn't resign from the Army Air Corps, so they assigned him to load packages onto a "Federal Express type" airplane (before there was Federal Express) that carried packages all over the world. He and the two pilots were the only people onboard the plane. They flew wherever they were instructed to go. My friend never did learn to fly.

I was asked why I didn't quit. Honestly, it never occurred to me to resign from the flight program. One of the things Dad had always taught me was to see things through to the end. And I felt the Lord had placed me in the Army Air Corps for a reason, and I was here to stay.

Evelyn followed me to Tulare by a later train and rented a room from a nice family. I couldn't live off base, but we could spend the weekends together.

I spent three months at the academy learning to fly a Stearman biplane with an open cockpit. I had one bad experience flying the plane. While learning to jump a fence, I punched a hole in the wing. The wings were fabric covered and easy to repair.

Air Cadet J.C. Martin, Jr. with Stearman biplane

J.G. "Tex" Rankin, the academy's namesake, was already one of the nation's most famed stunt pilots and flight school instructors when war clouds began gathering around the nation in 1940.

With World War II raging in Europe and the Japanese threatening on the other side of the world, Rankin felt that conflict was imminent and that the nation had better ready itself by turning out a new generation of pilots. He was operating the Rankin School of Flying at the Los Angeles Metropolitan Airport when he began scouting for places to train budding fighter aces.

Rankin first chose Bakersfield as a likely site but was turned down by Army officials because of its proximity to another airfield. He veered north to Delano, and signals from the military about the location were optimistic as well. Then a Tularean named Don Cornell intervened. Cornell, an old friend and manager of what was then Tulare Airpark, contacted Rankin and urged him to visit Tulare, which became the final choice for the flight-training center. But the airpark was located in the way of radio beams. A compromise was then struck for a huge plot of land four miles east on the destitute alkali flats on Tulare's fringe.

With the site secured, financing was the next hurdle. The city, helped by enthusiastic citizens, raised $300,000 to buy 560 acres of land and underwrite installment of services such as water and power. Ground was broken on February 12, 1941. It is more accurate to say that mud was plowed on the site, since it rained 45 of the next 60 days of construction, turning the field into a quagmire.

Money also continued to be a problem. Unexpected expenses cropped up but were all dealt with in time for the Rankin Aeronautical Academy to open for its first classes in April 1941.

There were 41 aspiring airmen in that first class.

The war on each side of the world provided Rankin and his instructors with plenty of business for the next four years. The flight center trained a total of 10,450 cadets, of which more than 8,000 graduated.

Their skills drawn from Rankin and his top-notch staff of instructors spoke for themselves. Those pilots who learned their craft in Tulare collected 6,820 medals for their war efforts, and 12 earned "ace" status for downing five or more enemy planes.

Rankin's most famous graduate was Maj. Richard I. Bong, also known as "Bing Bang" Bong, who shot down 40 enemy planes in the Pacific Theater, the most of any American pilot.

The activity at Rankin Field through those years was hectic. Those cadets logged a total of 584,500 hours flown, or the equivalent of 67 straight years in the air. Mechanics also kept pace with the volume of flying activity. During Rankin's tenure, there were 1,121 engines installed, 81,800 spark plugs changed, and 3,696 tires gone through.

Tulare Historical Museum houses much of Rankin Academy's history in its Military Wing, as well as many archives in the Tom Hennion Archives Center.

Our Class of 1944-E celebrated our completion of training at a Graduation Dance on January 5, 1944. We were part of the Fourth Army Air Force Flying Training Detachment.

Evelyn & Joe Carl, Jr.

Rankin Aeronautical Academy
L-R: J.G. Langdon, Instructor; V.L. Merriman; H.E. Mikoloyck; R.A. Marinconz; J.C. Martin, Jr.; R.L. Minton.

Next stop, Merced Army Air Field.

Chapter 5

Flying is hours and hours of boredom
sprinkled with a few seconds of sheer terror.
~ Gregory "Pappy" Boyington

Earning My Wings
(1944)

Merced Army Air Field ~ Vultee Vibrator

From Rankin Aeronautical Academy, I went to Merced Army Air Field, about 100 miles northwest of Tulare, where I learned to fly the BT-13 trainer, an all-metal, single-wing aircraft named the Vultee BT-13 Valiant. We cadets called it the Vultee Vibrator, because it vibrated violently when you reached stalling speed and went out of control. This was one of the first things we learned in order to control the plane when it stalled. We lost several planes in my Class of 1944 because of this problem.

BT-13 at Minter Field, CA, March 1943
~ https://www.wmof.com/bt-13.html

We also learned how to use a plane's instruments to land in the fog that rolled in off the Pacific Ocean. All airplanes have six basic instruments: airspeed indicator, attitude indicator, altimeter, turn coordinator, heading indicator, and vertical speed indicator. Using these instruments to monitor an airplane's position, rather than outside visual references, is known as attitude instrument flying.

Our instructors were Army Air Force officers, and, since we were lowly cadets, they treated us with contempt. I met my instructor several times in town, and he would not even look at me when I saluted him. He acted like he was mad at the world. Maybe he was. Maybe he wanted to be over in

Europe where the fighting was and not stuck in California teaching cadets how to fly. I don't know, but I was glad he was there. I learned a lot about flying.

First known as Air Corps Basic Flying School, Merced, in September 1941, it was renamed Merced Army Air Field in April 1942. It became one of the fields utilized to meet the needs of the 30,000 Pilot Training Program, providing basic air training for beginning pilots and crewmen, including a number of Women Airforce Service Pilots (WASP).

In 1942, as the country reeled from the attack on Pearl Harbor, trained male pilots were in short supply. Qualified pilots were needed to fight the war. The Army

On Christmas Eve 1944, Brig. Gen. Frederick Castle rode his flaming B-17 to his death while leading the biggest bombing mission of World War II during the Battle of the Bulge. He was air commander and leader of more than 2,000 heavy bombers in a strike against German airfields on 24 December 1944. He was posthumously awarded the Medal of Honor for his heroic action. The former Merced Army Air Field was renamed Castle Field in his honor on 17 January 1946. With the establishment of the US Air Force, the field was renamed Castle Air Force Base effective 13 January 1948.

~ https://www.militarymuseum.org/CastleAFB.html

tested aircraft that had been repaired before the men were allowed to fly them again. For over two years, the WASP went on to perform a wide variety of aviation-related jobs and to serve at more than 120 bases around the country.

~ https://www.waspmuseum.org/
~ https://www.lonestarflight.org/

Female pilots, from left, Frances Green, Margaret (Peg) Kirchner, Ann Waldner, and Blanche Osborn, walk from their aircraft at Lockbourne Army Air Force Base in Ohio during World War II. The four were members of a group of Women Airforce Service Pilots trained to ferry the B-17 Flying Fortresses.

~ https://ww2.stripes.com/epaper/special-publications/wasp

At the peak of the cadet program, the school graduated 1,000 cadets every five weeks, with approximately 13,000 cadets receiving training at Merced Army Flying School. The school had 600 assigned aircraft, of which 525 flew daily.

Marfa Army Air Field ~ Cessna AT-17

After three months of training at Merced Army Air Field, I was sent back to Texas to the Marfa Army Air Field. Planning for the construction of Marfa AAF began in March 1942, when the War Department selected the Marfa, Texas, area as a site for training United States Army Air Corps advanced twin-engine pilots. The Southern Pacific Railroad tracks ran parallel to Route 90 in that area, and the highway and railroad provided excellent logistics support for the new airfield.

The small town of Marfa had two hotels and a few homes. The hotels were booked solid every weekend, so Evelyn and I could only book a hotel room every other week. There were not enough places for the wives or girlfriends to stay, so the base built small barracks to rent to them because they needed the women to work on the base. We could walk over and visit our wives or girlfriends during our free time.

> *Marfa is a city in the high desert of the Trans-Pecos in far West Texas, located between the Davis Mountains and Big Bend National Park. The Marfa Army Air Field served as a training facility for several thousand pilots during World War II, including the American actor Robert Sterling, before closing in 1945. The base was also used as the training ground for many of the United States Army's chemical mortar battalions.*
>
> *Various movie productions have filmed in and around parts of Marfa—the 1950 film "High Lonesome," as well as the 1956 Warner Bros. film "Giant." Director George Stevens actively encouraged the townspeople to visit the set, either to watch the shooting, visit with the cast and crew, or take part as extras, dialect coaches, bit players, and stagehands.*
>
> *~ https://en.wikipedia.org/wiki/Marfa,_Texas*

I learned to handle a twin-engine plane, most of which were five-passenger Cessna AT-17s. The frame was made of steel, and the tail and wings were wood, all covered with fabric over wood skinning, which made for a light plane and was good for training.

After three months at Marfa Army Air Field, we took our final round-trip flight to Amarillo, Texas. Two pilots to each plane, one flew the plane and the other navigated. We hit a dust storm that we couldn't get over and had to fly through. We got lost for a while, which burned too much fuel. The low fuel light came on, which meant there was only 30 minutes of fuel left. So, we landed in a small corn field, about 15 miles short of the Amarillo Army Air Field.

We found a phone at a nearby farm, and I called our instructor. He flew over and brought us fuel. The other pilot was afraid to try to take off in such a short distance. There was no runway, only a grassy field. So, I took the controls and took off without any trouble.

Five-Passenger Cessna AT-17

One other incident occurred while I was at Marfa Army Air Field. One of the pilots was flying solo, got lost, and crossed the Rio Grande into Mexico. He ran out of fuel and landed in a Mexican farmer's field. It took the Army 30 days to find him.

Graduation Day

2nd Lt. Joe Carl Martin, Jr.

Graduation day finally arrived on May 23, 1944. We were promoted to officers in the United States Army Air Forces with the rank of Second Lieutenant, received our Wings, and were certified as pilots. It was a proud day. I had my Wings and my beautiful wife applauding from the stands. My base pay was now $118 a month.

Our celebration was short-lived, though. We left the next day for training in B-17 bombers.

Because Mother was unable to travel to the graduation ceremony, my parents received the following letter from my Commanding Officer, Colonel Donald B. Phillips:

"Your son received his wings today. It was a big day for him, as it was for you. It marked the culmination of many months of intensified, diligent, and self-sacrificing work.

"Because the difficulties of war-time travel make it impracticable for many parents to be present at today's commencement exercises, I am taking this means of congratulating you, hoping that the enclosed news releases and pictures of your son will bring the graduation a little closer to your home.

"From Marfa, your son goes on to further prepare himself for the job ahead.

"We at the pilot school, like you, are proud of him."

Chapter 6

Offense is the essence of air power.
~ General H.H. "Hap" Arnold USAAF

Flying Fortress (1944)

Fighting the Axis

In 1939, as war in Europe began to escalate, the commanding general of the U.S. Army Air Corps, Major General Henry "Hap" H. Arnold, was faced with a serious problem. Arnold realized that if the United States entered the war, it would take a major commitment in both money and manpower to build enough military facilities and train enough men to build an air force that would be successful against the Axis powers. By 1940, Arnold was able to convince military planners that to win a war in Europe it would be necessary to upgrade facilities and train more pilots and flight crews—and they needed to do it fast. To put their plan into action, the Army reorganized their aeronautical division, changing its name from Air Corps to Air Forces.

> *By 1943, the peak year of construction activity, the AAF had built 783 airfields (including subbases and auxiliary fields), and by the end of the war had graduated 224,331 pilots.*
> *~ https://www.hobbsnm.org/files/engineering/planning/haaf_history.pdf*

Hobbs Army Air Force Base

The City of Hobbs, New Mexico, actively solicited the AAF to consider their small community on New Mexico's southeastern plains as a potential site for an air-training center. The city touted the wide-open natural environment and ideal year-round flying conditions as features suited to the Army's aviation needs.

The attack on Pearl Harbor on December 7, 1941, and the subsequent declarations of war, hastened the Army's need for training bases. On December 18, 1941, Major John Armstrong, commander of the Roswell Army Air Field, visited Hobbs to conduct a preliminary investigation of potential sites around the city and to discuss the matter with city, political, and business leaders.

The 3,066-acre Hobbs Army Air Force Base (HAAF) was designed according to a standardized plan, consisting of three main parts: (1) a cantonment area, (2) a supply Sub-Depot, and (3) the flight line, runways, and taxiways.

Except for the Women's Army Air Corps (WAAC) two-story barracks, the living quarters for enlisted men and officers were all one story, were poorly insulated, and did not have central heating or indoor plumbing.

The first class of 80 cadets for bombardier school arrived on September 7, 1942. On November 21 of that year, the first and only class of the bombardier school graduated from the HAAF. Halfway into their training, they learned that the airfield's mission was to change to become a specialized four-engine pilot transition school where pilots would be trained to fly the AAF's long-range bomber, the B-17 Flying Fortress.

"Handsome and wonderfully reliable, the Boeing B-17 Flying Fortress had four engines, a cruising speed of 190 mph, weighed 50,000 pounds, and could carry six tons of bombs 1,200 miles. With thirteen .50-caliber machine guns for armament, the aerial battleship was one of the most effective bombers ever built."

~ Cervantes, Henry, Lt. Col. USAF (Ret.) Piloto: Migrant Worker to Jet Pilot, © 2007 (51)

H.H. Arnold, General, U.S. Army,
Commanding General, Army Air Forces
"Wings Over America," Hobbs Army Air Force Yearbook, 1943

"As members of the United States Armed Forces, you do not have to be told of the magnitude and importance of the task that lies before you.

"At every base, station, and training field of the United States Army Air Forces, you are preparing yourselves for the great test of arms, which will prove that the forces of democracy can destroy the evil power of the totalitarian nations.

"Soon you will take your places as Bombardiers, Navigators, Pilots, and Gunners alongside of our allies who have been fighting so valiantly. As mechanics and supply personnel, and in every type of ground duty, you have the vital responsibility of making sure that our airplanes will be second to none.

"We can win this war, and we will win it, but only if every officer and enlisted man puts forth all the fortitude and resourcefulness that Americans have always displayed in time of war.

"There are trying times ahead, times that will test the mettle of all of us, but I am confident that the personnel of my command will acquit themselves with honor and distinction, no matter where and when we shall meet the enemy."

~ http://www.hobbshistory.com/HAAFYearbook/index.html

Command of the Air

As noted in *Masters of the Air* by Donald L. Miller, American airpower was born during World War I, and Brigadier General William "Billy" Mitchell was its prophet. Mitchell was born in Nice, France, on December 29, 1879, while his parents were on vacation. He was fluent in French as well as English. He grew up in Milwaukee and attended Racine College and Columbian University (now The George Washington University in Washington, D.C.). Before graduation, however, he enlisted in the 1st Wisconsin Infantry in 1899 as a private to fight in the Spanish American War. After the war ended, he stayed in the U.S. Army Signal Corps and served in Cuba and the Philippines during the Philippine Insurrection.

Sent to Alaska in 1901, Mitchell distinguished himself by successfully laying a telegraph line through some of the most remote parts of that territory. While stationed in Alaska, Mitchell studied Otto Lilienthal's glider experiments, and he wrote an article in 1906 predicting that wars would soon be fought in the air and under the sea.

After attending the Army Staff College, Mitchell became the only Signal Corps officer on the Army General Staff in 1913. Since Army aviation was assigned to the Signal Corps, Mitchell became familiar with the early military aviators. In 1916, the year he learned to fly at the late age of 37, he was appointed chief of the U.S. Army Signal Corps's tiny Aviation Section, the first American air force. Two years later, he organized and led the overseas section of the U.S. Army's new Air Service, the larger organization that replaced the Aviation formed in 1926. Mitchell would achieve his greatest fame as an advocate of new ideas about airpower.

During World War I, Mitchell's first experience was the transforming event of his life. Living in the trenches with the infantry, he had an opportunity to fly over the enemy's positions with a French pilot. "We could cross the lines of these contending armies in a few minutes in our airplane," he wrote, "whereas the armies had been locked in the struggle, immobile, powerless to advance, for three years." As Mitchell saw it, "the art of war had departed. Attrition, or the gradual killing off of the enemy, was all the ground armies were capable of."

When General John "Black Jack" J. Pershing arrived in France as commander of the American Expeditionary Forces, Mitchell approached him with a daring proposal: use airpower to strike the Germans behind their lines, knocking out airfields and sources of supply. In the last months of the war, when American airpower had been built up from nothing to something of consequence—750 planes, fully 10 percent of the Allied effort—Pershing allowed Mitchell to use massed Allied fighter and bomber forces to support two major infantry offenses at St. Mihiel and the Meuse-Argonne.

"The air offensive which Mitchell laid on in the Meuse-Argonne in September [1918] was the greatest thing of its kind seen in the war," Hap Arnold wrote in his memoirs. "Until then, the air fighting had been chiefly between individual pilots . . . [This] was the first massed air striking power ever."

A West Point graduate, Hap Arnold was one of the Army's first of four licensed pilots, having been taught to fly by the Wright brothers, Orville and Wilbur, at their Dayton, Ohio, flying school. Friends called him "Hap," short for Happy, because he had an enigmatic smile permanently fixed on his face, but that benign countenance hid a volcanic temper and a crusading desire to advance the cause of American military aviation. He was one of the first and most enthusiastic of Billy Mitchell's supporters.

Mitchell drew his ideas from many sources. One of them was the Italian air commander General Giulio Douhet. The experience of World War I was paramount. Mitchell and Douhet both sought to end long wars of attrition and close-quarter slaughter. They proposed to shorten the war by returning the advantage to the offensive. Advances in the technology of killing—the machine gun, poison gas, and rifled artillery—had made infantry attacks on dug-in positions suicidal. The solution they arrived at independently was airpower—Winged Victory.

Just as technology had swung the advantage to the defense, now it would favor the offense. The airplane, the greatest offensive weapon yet developed, would break the supremacy of the defense. At a time when German strategists, in reaction to the static war they had just lost, were secretly developing a new form of warfare based on quick-striking tanks and armored vehicles, Mitchell and Douhet were advancing ideas for blitzkrieg warfare from the skies.

Douhet insisted that future wars would be short, total, and "violent to a superlative degree." They would be won from the skies with vast fleets of long-range bombers. The winning side would be the one that attacked first and without cease, gaining command of the air, not primarily by destroying the enemy's air force in combat but by destroying its air bases, communications, and centers of production.

Long-Range Bomber

On May 24, 1944, the day after graduation, we left by train from Marfa Army Air Field and headed to Hobbs Army Air Force Base in New Mexico. We were to learn how to fly the Boeing four-engine B-17 known as the Flying Fortress.

2nd Lt. Joe Carl Martin, Jr. & a B-17G

Learning to fly a B-17 was a huge change, compared to what I'd been piloting. The first time I saw a B-17, it looked like a monster to me. I would be responsible for eight other men who were going to climb into this big bomber with me and trust me to get them home. I had a lot to learn.

The training goals were simple: train the pilots and move them to the combat zones as quickly as possible. The instructors had nine weeks to graduate each incoming class. A pilot's training day ran from 6:00 am to midnight and included long-distance weekend flights that lasted at least 10 hours. A cadet's total flying time over the nine weeks was 105 hours, including instrument training and formation flying.

After about a month of flying this big plane, I thought I was a real hotshot. While learning to land close and short, my instructor kept after me to land closer to him, so I did. One day, I was right on his tail, and he stopped too quickly. My copilot put up the flaps, and our plane picked up speed. I ran over my instructor's plane and sheared off one wing from both planes. No one was hurt, except for our pride, including the instructor. The review board we had to go before was none too pleased, but they gave us another chance to get it right.

My biggest problem while stationed at Hobbs was finding the runway at night. The area was covered with new oil wells, and, when they burned off the natural gas, it produced flares that were in a straight line for miles and looked like our runway.

On one training mission, we made a long flight to the East Coast and back nonstop with several pilots taking turns flying. As with most planes flown during WWII, crewmembers dealt with very cold flights in unpressurized cabins, with temperature gauges in the cockpit frequently reading minus 40 degrees Fahrenheit. Crews stayed warm in fleece-lined uniforms.

After three months of training, I received orders to take a ten-day leave, and then I was to report to Lincoln Army Air Field in Nebraska, which was about an hour's drive southwest of Omaha.

Before leaving Houston, I had purchased a badly used 1939 Ford 2-door sedan from an oil company. While I was earning my wings, Mr. Rohrer had repaired and painted the car. George, his son and my good friend, was in the Navy, so Mr. Rohrer drove my car to Norman, Oklahoma. Evelyn took the bus from Hobbs to Norman to get the car from Mr. Rohrer, and then she drove back to Hobbs to be with me. We received fuel stamps so we could buy gas for the car and drove home to Houston for my ten-day leave.

Dad, Mother, Tomalene, and me.

We blew a tire on the way and had no ration stamps to buy a new tire. But people went out of their way to help soldiers, and we made it home without any more problems.

We visited with both of our parents, knowing this would be the last time I would see them before going overseas to fight in the war.

Then Evelyn and I headed to Lincoln, Nebraska.

Nebraska WWII army airfields were major USAAF training centers for pilots and aircrews of USAAF fighters and bombers during WWII. Nebraska was favored because it has excellent, year-round flying conditions. The sparsely populated land made ideal locations for gunnery, bombing, and training ranges. The training that was given to the airmen stationed at these airfields gave them the skills and knowledge that enabled them to enter combat in all theaters of warfare and enabled the Allies to defeat Nazi Germany and Imperial Japan.

~ https://en.wikipedia.org/wiki/Nebraska_World_War_II_army_airfields

Chapter 7

My soul finds rest in God alone; my salvation comes from Him.
He alone is my rock and my salvation; He is my fortress.
I will never be shaken. ~ Psalm 62:1-2 (NIV)

Becoming an Airplane Commander (1944)

Meeting My Crew

After I reported in at Lincoln Army Air Field in June 1944, I was promoted to First Lieutenant and met the crew I would go overseas with.

- Copilot: Warrant Officer Henry "Hank" Cervantes
- Navigator: 2nd Lt. Antonio "Tony" Picone
- Togglier (Bombardier)/Nose Gunner: S/Sgt. Ralph Spada (We didn't carry a bomb sight. Spada dropped the bombs on a signal from the Lead Plane. From his position in the Plexiglas nose of the plane, he had a switch to open the bomb bay doors and a toggle switch to release the bombs.)
- Radio Operator/Gunner: Sgt. Norman Larsen
- Ball Turret Gunner: Sgt. Celeste "Les" Rossi (He transferred out of our crew after a few missions. Rossi received an offer to learn how to operate a new type radar used to scramble the radar on anti-aircraft guns. Rossi was replaced by Cpl. Alfred S. Collins.)
- Tail Gunner: S/Sgt. Paul Gerling
- Waist Gunner: S/Sgt. Matthew "Matt" Schipper (the oldest man on the crew, age 28)
- Top Turret Gunner/Engineer: T/Sgt. William "Dude" E. Dudecz

In the B-17 Pilot Training Manual, 1943, in part it states:

Your assignment to the B-17 airplane means that you are no longer just a pilot. You are now an airplane commander, charged with all the duties and responsibilities of a command post.

You are now flying a 10-man weapon [changed to 9 crewmen June 7, 1944]. It is your airplane and your crew. You are responsible for the safety and efficiency of the crew at all times—not just when you are flying and fighting, but for the full 24 hours of every day while you are in command.

Your crew is made up of specialists. Each man—whether he is the navigator, bombardier, engineer, radio operator, or one of the gunners—is an expert in his line. But how well he does his job, and how efficiently he plays his part as a member of your combat team, will depend to a great extent on how well you play your own part as the airplane commander.

Your success as the airplane commander will depend in large measure on the respect, confidence, and trust which the crew feels for you. It will depend also on how well you maintain crew discipline.

Train your crew as a team. Keep abreast of their training. It won't be possible for you to follow each man's course of instruction, but you can keep a close check on his record and progress.

Get to know each man's duties and problems. Know his job and try to devise ways and means of helping him to perform it more efficiently.

~ http://www.303rdbg.com/crew-duties.html

Rapid City Army Air Base

1st Lt. Joe Carl Martin, Jr.

Three months of training with my new aircrew at Lincoln Army Air Field gave me an opportunity to mature as a first lieutenant and airplane commander. I learned my crew's weaknesses as well as my own. I was their commander at all times, not their friend. Together, we learned what it meant to be part of something bigger than ourselves aboard a B-17.

Then our nine-man crew, along with other crews, took a train to Rapid City Army Air Base in South Dakota, where we were stationed from October through December 1944.

Evelyn drove our car to Rapid City, taking several of the wives and girlfriends with her. She located a motel that had small cabins with cooking facilities. As an officer, I was allowed to live off base, and, during that time, our first son was conceived. I learned nine months later that I was a father.

Joe Carl Martin III

Joe Carl Martin III was born on July 27, 1945, one month before I returned home from combat in Europe.

Evelyn and I spent Christmas in our little cabin paradise, and we had ham instead of turkey. The cabin didn't have a freezer, but it did have a screened-in enclosure on one of the windows to keep food items from cool to freezing.

During those three months of combat training at Rapid City, my crew and I learned formation flying, bombing procedures, and crew coordination. The gunners practiced shooting at objects on the ground and letting a temporary bombardier drop bombs using the Norden Bombsight.

The Norden Mk. XV, known as the Norden M series in Army service, was a bombsight used by the United States Army Air Forces (USAAF) and the United States Navy during World War II, and the United States Air Force in the Korean and Vietnam Wars. It was the canonical tachometric design, a system that allowed it to directly measure the aircraft's ground speed and direction, which older bombsights could only measure inaccurately with lengthy in-flight procedures. The Norden further improved on older designs by using an analog computer that constantly calculated the bomb's impact point based on current flight conditions, and an autopilot that let it react quickly and accurately to changes in the wind or other effects.

~ https://en.wikipedia.org/wiki/Norden_bombsight
~ https://masseyaero.org/news/Norden.html

I tried all the positions except the ball turret. I dropped bombs with the bombsight and fired the .50 caliber machine guns. I missed all the targets. I was much better at flying the plane. I will note here that none of the B-17s I flew during the war had a Norden Bombsight.

While living in South Dakota, I learned how to drive a car in the ice and snow. One night after night flying, I was driving to our cabin about midnight when the car stopped and wouldn't start. It was a lonely nine-mile walk to town. Another car came along, and the driver gave me a lift, taking me to my cabin where Evelyn was waiting up for me. When I got back to my car the next day, it started right up when I cranked the engine. I drove it to the gas station where I purchased my gas, and the station owner told me that the gas line had frozen due to condensation. He said I needed to put alcohol in the fuel tank each time I filled up, which I started doing, and I never had any more problems after that. In fact, one day, we drove the car to visit Mount Rushmore, a 30-minute drive southwest of Rapid City, and we had no problems at all.

Île de France

Right after Christmas 1944,

> *Majestic figures of George Washington, Thomas Jefferson, Theodore Roosevelt, and Abraham Lincoln, surrounded by the beauty of the Black Hills of South Dakota, tell the story of the birth, growth, development, and preservation of this country.*
> ~ https://www.nps.gov/moru/index.htm

we received orders to proceed back to Lincoln Army Air Field in Nebraska to complete our final processing for overseas duty, which included writing a last will and testament. For a 21-year-old, it was a sobering feeling to think that I might not return home. But, since becoming a Believer, my faith in the Lord Jesus Christ has never wavered. I didn't hesitate to serve my country, trusting in God and leaving my fate in His hands.

We were certified "Combat Ready" and put aboard a train that was headed to an unknown destination to board an unnamed ship that would take us to a theater of the war we had no knowledge of, for security reasons. The wives and girlfriends were sent home to wait and wonder about the fate of their men.

Back then, cars didn't have air conditioning, but we did have a heater, which was a little box under the dash without a windshield vent. Evelyn drove home to Texas with a candle on the dash to keep the windshield defrosted.

Several days later, it was dark when the train ground to a stop at our final destination—a dimly lit, wooden warehouse. With our bags in hand, we were rushed inside and lined up in rows. Red Cross ladies served us coffee and doughnuts, while GIs handed everyone a card with a number on it. Several doors on the opposite side of the warehouse opened. We picked up our bags and were shuffled out to a huge platform.

SS *Île de France*
~https://en.wikipedia.org/wiki/SS_%C3%8Ele_de_France

In the pitch-black darkness of night, it was hard to tell that we were facing the immense, grimy hull of a ship—the SS *Île de France*—a French passenger ship converted to carry troops and manned by the British Royal Navy.

Multiple streams of soldiers struggled up the gangways with their gear, and we joined them.

Aboard ship, sailors directed us to the cabin number printed on our respective cards. Officers were assigned to the top deck of the ship, where double-decked bunks were crammed into staterooms. Once I'd claimed my bunk, stowed my gear, and the ship was underway, we found out that we had just departed from the Boston Port of Embarkation.

The SS *Île de France* had been taken by the British when France fell to the German invasion of their country. It was now being used to move troops and war matériel. All the corridor walls had been covered over with plywood. In the more open interior areas, there were imprints on the walls where paintings used to hang. Anything reminiscent that the *Île de France* had once been a cruise ship had been removed or covered over.

The British operated the ship and the dining hall for the officers just like a cruise ship does today. The waiters were in formal dress, and we ordered from a menu. The tables had white tablecloths with crystal glasses and silver dinnerware, but I wasn't able to enjoy it. The officers' stateroom where my bunk was located was on the top deck. The ocean crossing was very rough, and the ship rocked continuously. One night the swells were so great, I almost fell out of bed. Except for the bar along the edge of the bunk, I would have.

The ship had had to make several sharp turns in the middle of the night, taking evasive action due to enemy submarines. This happened several times during the crossing. The ship sailed with her lights extinguished, especially at night, with blackout curtains covering all windows.

I became seasick at the first breakfast and was unable to go back to the dining hall for three days. I lived on oranges and chocolate bars that I bought in the Navy PX. I lay in my bed most of the time, but, by the third day, I felt better and went to check on my crew. But I couldn't find them in their assigned crew quarters. As I was walking around, I ran into my copilot, Hank Cervantes, who took me to the bottom of the ship. My aircrew had become friendly with some of the ship's crew. The British had invited my men to share their crew quarters and their food. There was a baked ham sitting on the table, and no one had been sick. The ship didn't rock down there. I would have stayed with them, but there wasn't enough room. So, I went back to my rocking bunk.

One day I went out on the "sun deck" to get some fresh air, but the sea was so rough, waves were coming over the bow. Again, I went back to my bunk. I realized that as long as I lay down, I would not get seasick. I took in just enough food to keep from starving and fluids to stay hydrated. And when I took my shower, salt water came out of the pipes. We were given special soap to use because of the water's salt content.

The SS *Île de France,* a passenger ship initially designed to carry 1,786 passengers, now carried a mix of more than 14,000 service men. When we first boarded the ship in Boston, we noticed some soldiers coming aboard in shackles. During our voyage, Hank met an Army lieutenant in the infantry who said this was his third trip overseas. He was the officer in charge of those men in shackles, who'd been arrested for desertion. The lieutenant was escorting those deserters to the front lines as part of the infantry.

Queen Mary

We didn't know to what area of the war we were headed, so the navigators broke out their sextants to find out where we were. The ship's captain took away their sextants, locking them up until we reached our destination.

RMS *Queen Mary*
~ http://RMSQueen Mary1Ship-HistoryandFacts(queenmarycruises.net)

On the seventh day of our rough transatlantic crossing, January 9, 1945, we found ourselves entering the Firth of Clyde into Glasgow, Scotland. As the SS *Île de France* made its approach to the dock, we could see the RMS *Queen Mary* anchored not far from us. A magnificent ocean liner, the *Queen Mary* had been converted into a troop ship to ferry allied soldiers for the duration of the war. It looked like a giant compared to the ship we were on.

In December 1942, the RMS Queen Mary carried 16,082 American soldiers from New York to Great Britain, a standing record for the most passengers ever transported on one vessel. During this trip, while 700 miles (1,100 km) from Scotland during a gale, she was suddenly hit broadside by a rogue wave that may have reached a height of 92 feet (28 meters). Dr. Norval Carter, part of the 110th Station Hospital on board at the time, wrote in a letter that at one point Queen Mary "damned near capsized. One moment the top deck was at its usual height and then, swoom! Down, over, and forward she would pitch." It was calculated later that the ship rolled 52 degrees and would have capsized had she rolled another 3 degrees. The incident inspired Paul Gallico to write his novel, "The Poseidon Adventure" (1969) and carry the incident to a fictional extreme. This was adapted as a 1972 film by the same name in which the SS Poseidon is turned upside-down, and the trapped passengers try to escape. Naturally, parts of the film were shot in the actual Queen Mary, conveniently docked in Long Beach, California.

~ https://en.wikipedia.org/wiki/RMS_Queen_Mary

Thorpe Abbotts Air Base

With our gear in tow, we disembarked from the *Île de France* to smaller boats that took us ashore and to waiting trains. Our orders were to report to the 100th Bomb Group at Thorpe Abbotts, an airfield on the east coast of England.

> *Thorpe Abbotts Airfield was an American bomber base some ninety miles north of London and a short stroll from the Norfolk hamlet that gave it its name. Station #139, as it was officially designated, with its 3,500 fliers and support personnel, was built on a nobleman's estate lands, and the crews flew to war over furrowed fields worked by Sir Rupert Mann's tenant farmers, who lived nearby in crumbling stone cottages heated by open hearths.*
>
> *A century or so behind London in its pace and personality, it had been transformed by the war into one of the great battlefronts of the world, a war front unlike any other in history.*
>
> *This was an air front . . . a new kind of warfare was being waged—high-altitude strategic bombing. It was a singular event in the history of warfare, unprecedented and never to be repeated.*
>
> *In the thin, freezing air over northwestern Europe, airmen bled and died in an environment that no warriors had ever experienced. It was an air war fought not at 12,000 feet, as in World War I, but at altitudes two and three times that, up near the stratosphere where the elements were even more dangerous than the enemy. In this brilliantly blue battlefield, the cold killed, the air was unbreathable, and the sun exposed bombers to swift violence from German fighter planes and ground guns. This endless, unfamiliar killing space added a new dimension to the ordeal of combat, causing many emotional and physical problems that fighting men experienced for the first time ever.*
>
> ~ *"Masters of the Air," © 2006, Donald L. Miller (1-2)*

We were now part of the Eighth United States Army Air Force, known as The Mighty Eighth, with approximately 68 air bases located throughout England. Forty of those bases were designated as heavy bombardment groups dedicated to either B-17s or B-24s. Thorpe Abbotts was a B-17 air base known as the 100th Bombardment Group with four bomb squadrons: 349th, 350th, 351st, and 418th. Our crew was assigned to the 349th Bomb Squadron.

Army trucks met us at the train station in London and took us to the base, where we arrived after dark. It was bitterly cold, and there was about a foot of snow on the ground. We were taken to some long, low concrete buildings and told to find an empty bunk for the night—officers in one building and everyone else in another building. There were plenty of empty bunks.

In the barracks, I received two Army blankets, a pillow (actually a straw-filled biscuit), and a cotton mattress on an Army cot for the duration. No sheets; there was a shortage. I was able to buy some sheets later from an officer who had finished his required number of missions and was headed home. We had a footlocker to store our clothes.

Thorpe Abbotts, Winter 1944-45
~ https://100thbg.com/ (Photo Gallery)

The following morning, we found out the reason for so many empty bunks. The 100th Bomb Group had lost all planes except one in the 349th Squadron that week.

One of the homebound veterans of the air war said that the 100th was a hard luck outfit. It was known as the "Bloody 100th" because the Luftwaffe had a vendetta against the group, repeatedly singling it out for attack.

German 88mm Flak Guns

Most of the planes were lost to German flak fired from 88mm flak guns. By 1943-44, the German flak defenses were equipped with efficient radar which gave precise data of enemy aircraft position and height. This information was processed through a Predictor (also known as a Director) which combined this information with other factors such as muzzle velocity, ambient temperature, wind direction, etc. This determined a coinciding position for shell and aircraft, giving the necessary bearing, fuse setting, and gun elevation. This was very complex, and dead time was a constant problem—the time it took for the gunner to set the fuse by hand, load, and fire, which nearly always varied.

The proximity fuse moved the game ahead considerably. To put it very simply, the fuse contained its own tiny radio transmitter. The fuse sent out a signal as the shell flew through the air, detonating upon receiving an echo back from its intended target—a B-17—and sending huge chunks of shrapnel into the plane's fuselage.

The price of freedom is never cheap—direct flak hit (This is NOT a 100th Bomb Group aircraft) ~ https://100thbg.com/ (Photo Gallery)

German 88mm flak gun in action against Allied bombers. ~https://en.wikipedia.org/wiki/Anti-aircraft_warfare

By January 1944, 20,625 flak guns were protecting the Reich, and a German flak officer estimated that 4,000 88mm shells were needed to down one bomber. By December 1944, it was estimated that German flak guns had fired 3,175,000 shells.

My crew was now part of the replacement crews for the B-17s of the 349th Squadron lost over Hamburg.

In the morning on the second day of our arrival, January 10, 1945, I started to walk to the flight line to see how it looked, and bombs started going off, shaking the ground and breaking windows in some of the buildings. I thought we were under attack, so I ran back to the barracks, because there was a bomb protection wall in front of our barracks. Someone came by and told me that a B-17 from another group was trying to make an emergency landing on our base, but it crashed into the bomb storage area. Bombs went off until after noon.

At the beginning of the war, 900 bombers a day darkened the skies over Germany. By the time our crew arrived in England, 1,200 bombers a day continued the relentless bombing of strategic targets. By the end of the war, 1,500 bombers a day finally forced Germany's surrender.

Unfortunately, President Franklin D. Roosevelt would not live to see the end of the war. Less than three months into his fourth term, he suffered a cerebral hemorrhage on April 12, 1945.

Harry S. Truman, during his few weeks as President Roosevelt's new vice president, scarcely saw the president and received no briefing on the development of the atomic bomb or the unfolding difficulties with Soviet Russia. Suddenly, these secret plans and a host of other wartime problems became Truman's to deal with when he became America's 33rd President.

Chapter 8

Courage is not the absence of fear;
it's the ability to act in spite of it.
~ Unknown

Missions Begin (January 1945)

Strategic bombing during World War II began on September 1, 1939, when Germany invaded Poland and the Luftwaffe (German Air Force) began bombing cities and the civilian population in Poland in an indiscriminate aerial bombardment campaign. As the war continued to expand, bombing by both the Axis and the Allies increased significantly. In September 1940, the Luftwaffe began targeting British cities in 'The Blitz.' From 1942 onward, the British bombing campaign against Germany became less restrictive and increasingly targeted industrial sites and, eventually, civilian areas. When the United States began flying bombing missions against Germany, it reinforced these efforts and controversial fire bombings were carried out against Hamburg (1943), Dresden (1945), and other German cities.
~ https://en.wikipedia.org/wiki/Strategic_bombing_during_World_War_II

Milk Runs

After our arrival at Thorpe Abbotts in January 1945, we went to classes to learn what to expect and to get our flying equipment that consisted of a flight suit, a Mae West life jacket, an electric heated suit, a flak suit, and a steel helmet with ear flaps. The flak suit was an armored vest made of cloth fabric filled with steel plates that resembled an over-sized catcher's chest protector that hung from our necks. My flight helmet came with earphones, goggles, a throat mike, and an oxygen mask. I also had an insulated suit with heavy insulated boots and a parachute. Each crewmember was issued a .45 caliber automatic pistol, shoulder holster, and waist holster.

We had to go to the PX to set up an account to purchase personal items, candy, cigarettes, and beer. I tried to opt out of the cigarettes and beer, since I didn't smoke or drink. But several men in line behind me convinced me to buy them to trade for other items among the crews. You were required to buy a month's supply at one time.

Once we were fully equipped, we flew practice missions around England to acquaint us with what to expect. Our first three flights were called "milk runs," because we had no enemy planes attacking us and very little flak hitting us. However, the men giving us our flight instructions failed to tell us about a small island off the coast of France that was occupied by German soldiers. Our squadron of nine planes flew over the island, and the Germans fired at us with cannons, hitting one ship. The shell put a hole through the center of the plane, but no one was hurt, and the shell did very little damage. We returned to base without any further incidents.

This had just been a practice mission, and our squadron had been fired on. Our real missions lay ahead—all 26 of them before we would be allowed to go home.

Squadron of 9 B-17s flying in formation.
~ https://100thbg.com/ (Photo Gallery)

A bombardment group or bomb group was a group of bomber aircraft in the United States Army Air Forces (USAAF) during World War II. It was the equivalent of an infantry regiment in the Army Ground Forces, or a bomber wing in the British Commonwealth air forces. A bombardment group was the key tactical control and administrative organization for bombers in all theaters of operation and was commanded by a colonel or lieutenant colonel.

U.S. bomb groups were numbered and classified into four types: Very Heavy (VH), Heavy (H), Medium (M), and Light (L). Groups that combined bombers of differing categories into a single administrative organization were designated "Composite" groups. Bomber aircraft were assigned to groups by category:

- *Very Heavy: B-29 Superfortress, B-32 Dominator*
- *Heavy: B-17 Flying Fortress, B-24 Liberator*
- *Medium: B-25 Mitchell, B-26 Marauder*
- *Light: A-20 Havoc, A-26 Invader*

By February 1945, the [USAAF] Heavy Bombardment Group of B-17s and B-24s consisted of 72 aircraft, 96 crews of 9 to 11 men per crew, of which there were 465 officers and 1,796 enlisted men for a total of 2,261 personnel.

The total complement of bombers was 309: Very Heavy Bombardment Group, 45; Heavy Bombardment Group, 72; Medium Bombardment Group, 96; and Light Bombardment Group, 96.

~ *https://en.wikipedia.org/wiki/Bombardment_group*

Our First Mission

We flew most of our missions in *E-Z Goin'*, a B-17G that answered to three-three-eight-five-one-four. Her official call sign was Kidmeat J-Jig. An unknown "nose-art" artist had emblazoned the name on her nose, and beneath it added a turtle with funny eyes and a gleeful smile, blithely hauling a bomb balanced atop its shell.

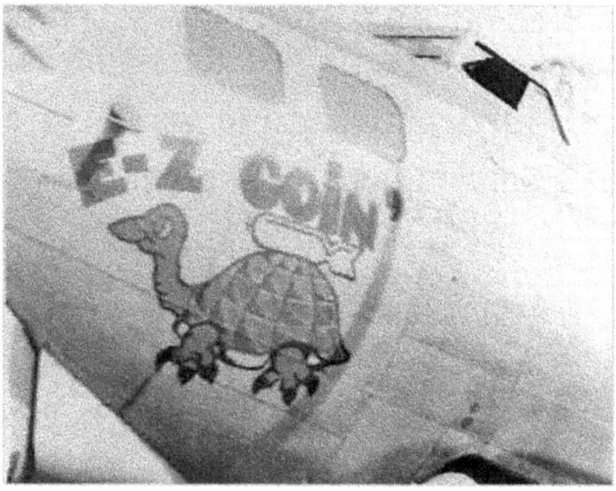

~ https://100thbg.com/ (Photo Gallery)

One of the other planes we flew was called *The Squawkin' Hawk.* She was the oldest bomber in the 100th. Rather than the natural metal finish of newer B-17s (like *E-Z Goin'*), it was pai nted creamed-coffee color with bright aluminum patches marking past wounds. The engines dripped oil and stenciled beneath the pilot's window were seven black swastikas.

~ https://100thbg.com/ (Photo Gallery)

✈ ✈ ✈

The following excerpt is a description of our first mission from *Piloto: Migrant Worker To Jet Pilot,* © 2007 (60-61, 62-63) by Lt. Col. Henry Cervantes, USAF (Ret.) and my former copilot "Hank." It is quoted here with his permission. Occasional remarks from me are noted in brackets.

"It was 0600, 19 February 1945. The skies were dark, cold sheets of water lashed across the ramp, and everything looked strange. Eight to ten B-17s were staggered on opposite sides of Runway 28, when a green-green flare arched high from the control tower. Immediately, four giant water rooster-tails spouted behind *FireBall Dog 1.* The heavily laden B-17 lumbered down the strip, broke ground, and rumbled out of sight. Precisely 25 seconds later, a second bomber went, then another, and another. Each departure set off a cacophony of screeching, squealing brakes, and engines roaring, alternating power blasts as the line of waiting planes moved forward. We reached the number one slot and Joe taxied ahead a bit. We locked the tail wheel, set the brakes, and gently coaxed the throttles full open. As the engines reached full song, blue fire poured from the superchargers and the plane began bouncing in its desire to fly. On the hack, Joe released the brakes and we had no sooner lifted off than we entered the clouds. Wheels up, flaps up, set climb power. We began a shallow left turn.

"We corkscrewed up and around a nearby radio beacon called Splasher 6 and emerged from billowing clouds at 12,000 feet. Soon the wing lights of all the 100th's thirty-six B-17s could be seen forming into four squadrons of nine aircraft each. As we continued to climb, the squadrons formed into one group layered and staggered horizontally and vertically. For the remainder of the flight, we maneuvered in unison with no space between us for zigzagging. By doing so, the amassed firepower of more than 430 closely spaced, heavy machine guns would contribute to the defense of the group.

"When the last B-17 was in place, the 100th joined the 90th and 390th

B-17s lined up for take-off.
~https://www.americanairmuseum.com/media/4687 (Roger Freeman Collection)

Bomb Groups to become the 13th Combat Wing. The formation commander then led his 108 B-17s to a designated spot within the 16 groups that comprised the 3rd Air Division. Up and down Bomber Alley, the 1st and 2nd Air Divisions formed in like manner, and nearly an hour after takeoff, the bomber stream made a sweeping turn east, and we headed toward so-called 'U.S. Highway 1', our usual flight path into Germany.

As a personal FYI, these long-range bombers did have bathroom facilities. A urination relief tube drained to a port on the outside of the aircraft, if the fluid didn't freeze and clog the tube. A chemical toilet (a bucket with a seat and cover) was located in the waist gunners' compartment. But using these receptacles wasn't practical under combat conditions and at minus 50° temps. While seated at our assigned positions, it was easier to pee into the condoms we carried for that purpose, since the fluid immediately froze into a solid mass, then you could roll the end into a tight knot and drop it to the floor. If unavoidable, we pooped in our wool underwear and worried about the smell and clean-up later, because that was the least of our worries.

~ Joe Carl Martin, Jr.

Formation Time ~Top view looking down

Formation Time ~ https://100thbg.com/ (Photo Gallery)

During the winter of 1944-45, minimizing losses to flak became a priority. The 27-plane box became standard for B-17s for all of 1945, spread more laterally to avoid catastrophic damage to the formation from a single shell burst. At the same time, wingmen flew more forward on element leaders, creating a box that was stacked 750 feet vertically, 650 feet from front to back, and 1,170 feet laterally. This final variation presented flak gunners with a small target, produced excellent bomb patterns, and was both easy to fly and control.

~ https://en.wikipedia.org/wiki/Combat_box

Combat Box

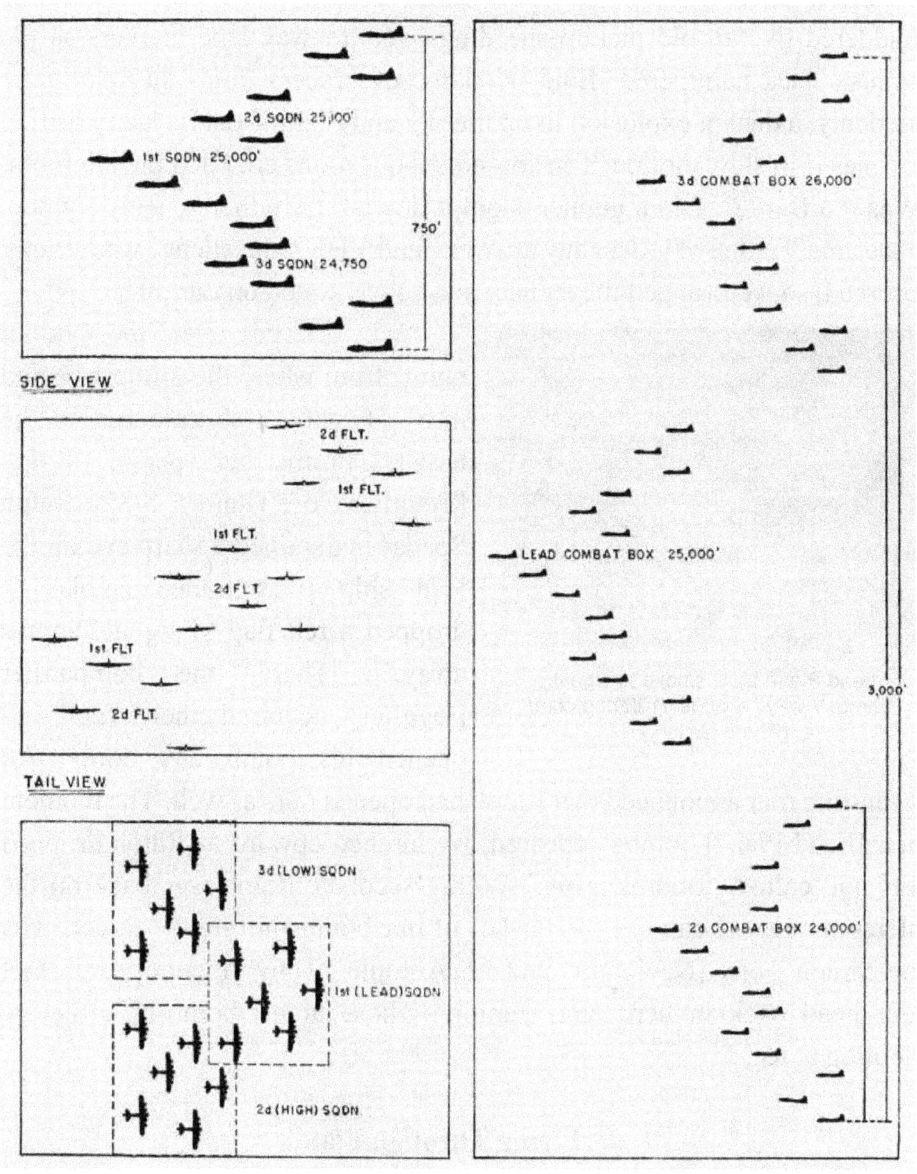

PLAN VIEW COMBAT BOX STAGGER COMBAT WING - THREE COMBAT BOXES

Typical group pattern of squadrons flying at different altitudes. We flew specific flight patterns so the bombs would be scattered out when dropped. The last and lowest group was in the vulnerable low squadron, known as the so-called Coffin Corner. Inexperienced pilots flew at the low level, while the most experienced pilots flew in the Lead Combat Box.

"Twenty minutes out over the North Sea, the VHF radio crackled, 'Gunners, cleared to test fire.' Our plane reeked of burning cordite and shuddered like an old pickup speeding over freeway lane markers as the gunners jack-hammered fluid streams of tracers into the darkness. Suddenly, a distant explosion lit up the sky and flaming debris lazily drifted down as if in slow motion. Tension-edged questions crowded the intercom, 'Was it a B-17?' 'Did a gunner shoot it down?' 'Are there enemy fighters in the area?' None of us had any answers, and VHF radio silence was strictly enforced, so we dropped the subject and concentrated on our jobs.

Lead Plane trails smoke to signal "Bombs Away." ~ https://100thbg.com/ (Photo Gallery)

"We arrived over the 'initial point' from where the group wheeled into a twenty-or-so-mile run to the target. From his perch, Ralph [Togglier/Nose Gunner, S/Sgt. Ralph Spada] maintained a sharp eye on the lead ship [that trailed smoke or dropped a red flag to signal 'bombs away.']. There, the bombardier [togglier] acquired the target and opened his bomb bay doors. An ocean-like roar announced that Ralph had opened ours as well. The moment their [Lead Plane] bombs appeared, we lurched upward as Ralph dropped ours and called, 'Bombs away.' Within seconds, Ralph was back on the intercom, 'Hey, I can see the flashes of our bombs hitting the target.' His companion Tony [Navigator, 2nd Lt. Antonio "Tony" Picone] said, 'Get your head back in here, you dummy. Those aren't bomb-hits, they're shooting at us.'

Flying Through Flak

"Puffs of black smoke shaped like little Casper the Friendly Ghosts dappled the sky around us. The tiny clouds seemed insignificantly small and incapable of creating all the horror stories we had heard. *Whumph! Whumph!* Suddenly, very nearby we saw two red flashes of fire, felt the concussions, and flak rattled off the paper-thin fuselage. Until that moment, the idea of going to war had a new and exciting feeling to it. Now I [Hank] felt naked; my knees met to protect my groin, my shoulders hunched, my elbows tucked in, and my neck shrank in an effort to hide my body under the flak suit. I also thought of removing my feet from the rudder pedals, but I already felt like a pretzel, and it is impossible to fly formation that way. I sat up and said to myself, 'To hell with it, if it's going to happen it's going to happen, do your job.' Hundreds of explosions blended into a dense cloud of greasy black smoke that we passed through and returned home. During debriefing, old hands judged the flak over the target as 'severe.'"

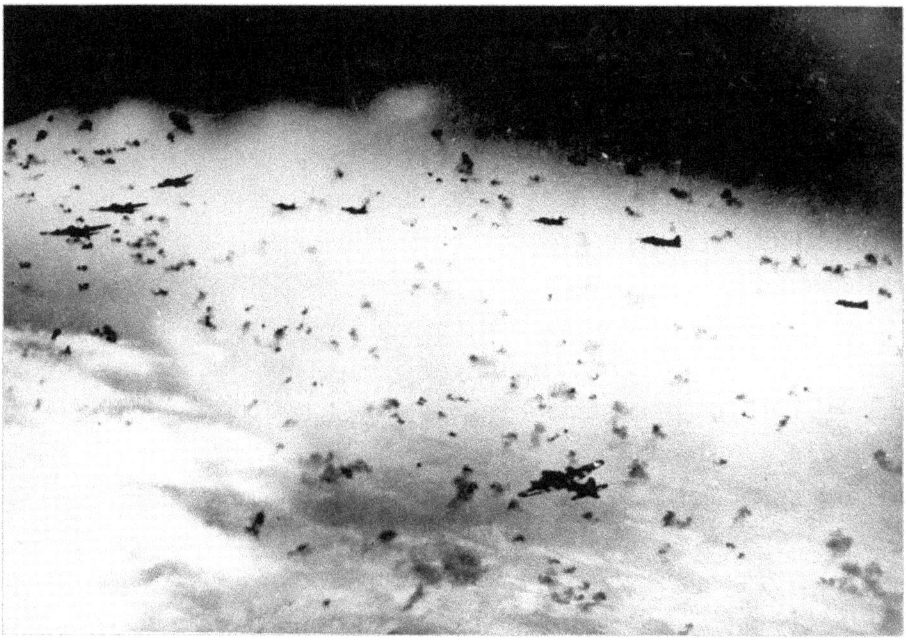
100th Bomb Group flying through heavy flak.
~ https://100thbg.com/ (Photo Gallery)

✈ ✈ ✈

Chapter 9

The Lord is the one who goes ahead of you; He will be with you. He will not fail you or forsake you. Do not fear or be dismayed.
~ Deuteronomy 31:8

Missions Intensify (February 1945)

Missions and Interrogations

Usually, on a mission, there would be 800 to 1,000 planes in the air. In order to assemble that many planes, the bomb groups (consisting of approximately 36 planes per group) stationed at various bases would take off at specific times during the early-morning dark, when most civilians were asleep, but I'm sure we woke them with the roar of our take-offs. We would follow a radio beacon, circling the beacon until all the bomb groups were assembled near England's east coast. Then we would proceed in formation across the North Sea to Germany. If for some reason, a bomb group could not keep the scheduled rendezvous, they were left behind or they could possibly cause mid-air collisions due to the darkness.

The Germans had a chain of radar stations that stretched from Norway to northern France, and they knew the Americans were coming from the time the planes began stacking up over East Anglia (east coast of England). As we crossed over the German border and passed over the neatly defined town of North-Rhine Westphalia, we began to run into intense antiaircraft fire, known as flak, a contraction of *Fliegerabwehrkanonen.* Flak shells were large mid-air grenades, bursting out at the seam along the shell, propelling shrapnel through the opening, and making it easier to take down a large object in the sky, like a B-17.

On one bombing run, German flak gunners were tracking *E-Z Goin'* and started shooting at us. My tail gunner called me on the intercom and said, "You better do something. They're getting closer." I said, "Okay, you let me know when they get a hundred yards behind us and I'll do something." Then he called back and said, "You better do it. The next one's going to hit us." We weren't allowed to break formation, but I could move the plane sideways, so I did. The shell went off near my left wing, with the shell exploding away from us, the concussion pushing us farther sideways. Then we moved back into formation.

We flew *through* flak. You couldn't dodge it, without taking out another B-17 and your bomber as well. One plane near mine was hit with flak and had a hole blown in it as big as a door. Some bombers hit by flak survived. During one instance, the big white star on the side of a B-17's fuselage was cut out by flak, which killed the radio operator, but that Flying Fortress kept flying.

There were no medics at 25,000 feet, no men wearing Red Cross brassards to rush to the aid of a shot-up crewmember. Fliers who knew almost nothing about first aid had to take care of each other, and themselves.

We'd continue on, in formation, to our Initial Point (IP)—the place where we'd line up for the bomb run on the assigned target, dropping tons of bombs in an effort to destroy the Nazis' ability to continue their war effort.

If a plane was damaged over German territory, they would lower their wheels then several German fighter planes would escort them down to a safe landing at a German-held base. Initially, the German pilots treated the downed crew very nicely, until they were turned over to the Gestapo and interned as prisoners of war.

Prisoners of War at Stalag Luft III

If you were lucky enough to survive parachuting from your disabled plane or landing on German soil and not get beaten to death by angry German civilians, you were marched with other downed crewmembers through the streets, past angry crowds that lined the sidewalks all the way to the train station you had just bombed. Your next stop would be Dulag Luft, the Luftwaffe's interrogation center, just outside Frankfurt. Upon arrival, the officers were put in solitary confinement and kept isolated from one another throughout their interrogations. You weren't really alone in your cramped, unheated cell. You usually had about a million fleas to keep you company.

After about nine days in solitary confinement and incessant rounds of interrogation, you were sent with other prisoners to Stalag Luft III, a prison camp for American and British air force officers in German-occupied Silesia, a former region of Poland.

Prisoners traveled in vile boxcars that had been used to haul livestock, and the smell of fresh manure was overwhelming. Since the transport of prisoners was given low priority, the cars were attached to one freight train after another and were often shunted off to railroad sidings. The 300-mile trip could take up to three days or more.

Stalag Luft III was in a thick pine forest just outside the small town of Sagan. It was only one of several prisoner of war camps where incarcerated airmen were fighting a different war—one of despair and survival, especially during the punishing winter of 1944-45.

By the end of the war, there were approximately 1,000 fliers of the 100th Bomb Group in German prison camps.

Real Scrambled Eggs

We flew in all kinds of weather—snow, rain, or sunny skies—all except fog, especially during take-offs. There was always a chance of crashing into another B-17. Forced to land in fog on instruments was the only exception. If we had to fly through fog or clouds, we used our searchlights fitted with red lenses at each window to alert other planes around us of our location to avoid collisions.

Contrails
~ https://100thbg.com/ (Photo Gallery)

We also had problems with flying at high altitude where the air is cooler than the heat coming off a B-17. The result causes contrails, which are clouds that form when water vapor condenses and freezes around small particles (aerosols) that exist in aircraft exhaust. Some of that water vapor comes from the air around the plane, and some is added by the exhaust of the aircraft that contains both gas (vapor) and solid particles. Contrails can be just as blinding as fog, to the point that you can't see the plane in front of you or beside you.

As part of the 349th Bomb Squadron, we were awakened at two in the morning to get ready for each day's mission. On my way to the mess hall, I'd stop in at the chapel to ask the Lord to help me bring my crew back safely. Then I'd continue on to the mess hall, where only the mission crews received real scrambled eggs for breakfast, along with flapjacks drenched in hot, caramel-colored syrup, greasy sausages, and black coffee. Lots of black coffee. Everyone else was served powered eggs. Sometimes, if I wasn't scheduled to fly a mission, I'd get up with those crews who were flying and eat breakfast in order to get fresh eggs, then I'd go back to bed.

When we returned from a mission, the first thing we did was go to interrogation, where they gave us a shot of whiskey to relax us. After the third mission, I decided I didn't need it and gave my shot of whiskey to one of the crew. Sometimes, the tail gunner was tipsy by the time the interrogation was finished.

Briefing Room, 8th Air Force
~ https://www.pinterest.com/annie1152/world-war-2/

Last Sound of the American Plane

For every scheduled mission, once we'd finished breakfast, the flying crews would assemble in the briefing room to get our assigned bombing targets. We knew where the concentration camps were located so we could avoid them. But, nearby the camps, there were German-held munitions plants, factories, or railroad yards where the camp prisoners were required to work, and that we were to bomb.

The following excerpt is from *Night* by Elie Wiesel and quoted here by permission of the publishers. *Night* is the first-person account of Eliezer "Elie" Wiesel of what occurred to him and his father as Jewish prisoners in Auschwitz and then Büchenwald concentration camps from May 1944 until April 11, 1945, when Büchenwald (near Weimer, Germany) was liberated by the U.S. Third Army. *Night*, © 1972, 1985, Elie Wiesel; Translation © 2006 by Marion Wiesel (58-61).

"One Sunday, as half of our group, including my father, was at work, the others, including me, took the opportunity to stay and rest.

"At around ten o'clock, the sirens started to go off. Alert. The *Blockälteste* gathered us inside the blocks, while the SS took refuge in the shelters. As it was relatively easy to escape during an alert—the guards left the watchtowers, and the electric current in the barbed wire was cut—the standing order to the SS was to shoot anyone found outside his block.

"In no time, the camp had the look of an abandoned ship. No living soul in the alleys. Next to the kitchen, two cauldrons of hot, steaming soup had been left unattended. Two cauldrons of soup! Smack in the middle of the road, two cauldrons of soup with no one to guard them! A royal feast going to waste! Supreme temptation! Hundreds of eyes were looking at them, shining with desire. Two lambs with hundreds of wolves lying in wait for them. Two lambs without a shepherd, free for the taking. But who would dare?

"Fear was greater than hunger. Suddenly, we saw the door of Block 37 open slightly. A man appeared, crawling snakelike in the direction of the cauldrons.

"Hundreds of eyes were watching his every move. Hundreds of men were crawling with him, scraping their bodies with his on the stones. All hearts trembled, but mostly with envy. He was the one who had dared.

"He reached the first cauldron. Hearts were pounding harder; he had succeeded. Jealousy devoured us, consumed us. We never thought to admire him. Poor hero committing suicide for a ration or two or more of soup. In our minds, he was already dead.

"Lying on the ground near the cauldron, he was trying to lift himself to the cauldron's rim. Either out of weakness or out of fear, he remained there, undoubtedly to muster his strength. At last, he succeeded in pulling himself up to the rim. For a second, he seemed to be looking at himself in the soup, looking for his ghostly reflection there. Then, for no apparent reason, he let out a terrible scream, a death rattle such as I had never heard before and, with open mouth, thrust his head toward the still steaming liquid. We jumped at the sound of the shot. Falling to the ground, his face stained by the soup, the man writhed a few seconds at the base of the cauldron, and then he was still.

"That was when we began to hear the planes. Almost at the same moment, the barrack began to shake.

"'They're bombing the Buna factory,' someone shouted.

"I anxiously thought of my father, who was at work. But I was glad nevertheless. To watch that factory go up in flames—what revenge! While we had heard some talk of German military defeats on the various fronts, we were not sure if they were credible. But today, this was real!

"We were not afraid. And yet, if a bomb had fallen on the blocks, it would have claimed hundreds of inmates' lives. But we no longer feared death, in any event not this particular death. Every bomb that hit filled us with joy, gave us renewed confidence.

"The raid lasted more than one hour. If only it would have gone on for ten times ten hours . . . Then, once more, there was silence. The last sound of the American plane dissipated in the wind and there we were, in our cemetery. On the horizon, we saw a long trail of black smoke. The sirens began to wail again. The end of the alert.

"Everyone came out of the blocks. We breathed in air filled with fire and smoke, and our eyes shone with hope. A bomb had landed in the middle of the camp, near the *Appelplatz*, the assembly point, but had not exploded. We had to dispose of it outside the camp.

"The head of the camp, the *Lagerälterest*, accompanied by his aide and by the chief *Kapo*, were on an inspection tour of the camp. The raid had left traces of great fear on his face.

"In the very center of the camp lay the body of the man with soup stains on his face, the only victim. The cauldrons were carried back to the kitchen.

"The SS were back at their posts in the watchtowers, behind their machine guns. Intermission was over.

"An hour later, we saw the *Kommandos* returning, in step as always. Happily, I caught sight of my father.

"'Several buildings were flattened,' he said, 'but the depot was not touched . . .'

"In the afternoon, we cheerfully went to clear the ruins."

Büchenwald concentration camp. Photo taken April 16, 1945, five days after liberation of the camp. Sixteen-year-old Wiesel is in the second row from the bottom, seventh from the left, next to the bunk post.

~ https://en.wikipedia.org/wiki/Elie_Wiesel

> *"The smell of death overwhelmed us even before we passed through the stockade. More than 3,200 naked, emaciated bodies had been flung into shallow graves. Others lay in the streets where they had fallen.... [General] Eisenhower's face whitened into a mask. [General] Patton walked over to a corner and sickened. I was too revolted to speak. For here death had been so fouled by degradation that it both stunned and numbed us...."*
>
> *~ General Omar N. Bradley from "World War II Reminiscences" by Colonel John H. Roush, Jr. © 2013 (385)*

Chapter 10

And Jesus said, "I am the resurrection and the life;
he who believes in Me will live even if he dies."
~ John 11:25

Losing Friends (March 1945)

New Type of German Plane

On March 3, 1945 (our 7th mission), the 100th led the mission of over 1,000 bombers to Germany. As part of the 349th Squadron, we flew ahead of the bomb group, dropping "chaff" (small strips of foil made from aluminum). It confused the radar on the German antiaircraft guns. We'd been warned that a new type of German plane might be sighted. This new plane had no prop. It was jet powered, but we didn't know what it looked like.

The Germans had a new, twin-engine, swept-wing fighter called the Messerschmitt Me-262. ~ https://acepilots.com/german/me262_17.jpg

I was flying to the left and behind the lead aircraft when a plane, a swastika on its tail, came from out of nowhere and slowed down next to my left wing. I could see the pilot's face, and he gave me a figure wave. I called for the gunners to shoot him, but it was too late. He shot down the Lead Plane piloted by 2nd Lt. Jack W. Thrasher. The German jet went straight up out of sight before anyone could get a gun on him.

✈ ✈ ✈

The following excerpt is from *Piloto: Migrant Worker To Jet Pilot,* © 2007 (68-69) by Lt. Col. Henry Cervantes, USAF (Ret.) and my former copilot "Hank." It is quoted here with his permission. Occasional remarks from me are noted in brackets.

"*Pow-pow-pow-pow-pow!* Smoking cannon shells stitched bright jagged holes across Jack's left wing. Flames erupted and Jack side-slipped the plane in an effort to douse the blaze. That didn't help, so he returned to straight-and-level flight and the fire intensified. As expected, crewmen came tumbling out of the escape hatches; one, two, three, four, five, six—six—six, *boom!* The plane exploded with Jack still visible at the controls. He and two men died.

"When a stricken B-17 plunged to earth, it usually dived or spiraled down with a certain elegance that glossed over the fact that inside, terrorized men were reeling around like dice in a tin cup. When one exploded, however, huge assemblies, parts and pieces, and flaming fuel and oil flew off in all directions, and the crew was blasted into space like so many scarecrows! As we staggered through the shock wave, I [Hank] caught my breath, my stomach muscles knotted, my body went rigid, and I got goose bumps. A moment later, nothing! All traces of the explosion were behind us, and we were flying formation with a hole in the sky.

Loss formation.
~ https://100thbg.com/ (Photo Gallery)

"Dismayed, Joe and I glanced at one another then looked away. One never felt more alive than when he had cheated death, and it was embarrassing to find yourself elated when friends were dying. You felt a need to apologize to someone—anyone—for them being killed and you being spared.

"The horror of a fire at altitude never fades. The air is so clear up there that fire appears brighter and deadlier than on the ground. It is the death fliers fear most, and the memory remains coiled and ready to strike when least expected. Don't ever let some macho pilot tell you he doesn't know the meaning of the word *fear*. All who fly have had full-body bear hugs with it. As they say, however, 'The difference between pilots is their ability to handle fear. And if you can't, you shouldn't be one.'"

Jack W. Thrasher Crew (left to right) Standing: Jack Thrasher (P), Ernest Coble (CP), Maurice Kay (BOM), Gerald Rimmel (NAV). Kneeling: Albert Egsieker (ROG), Joseph Turrenne (WG), Cecil Baker (TG), Thomas Browning (TTE), George Mensler (NG). Photo courtesy of Sally Browning Holloway, daughter of Thomas Browning. According to Jack O'Leary (20 Jan 2005), this photo was taken on 25 Oct 1944 at Ardmore AAF, Oklahoma. 2nd Lt. Maurice Kay was removed from the Thrasher crew after training in the States and was replaced by Cpl. George Mensler. ~ https://100thbg.com/ (Photo Gallery)

Greater love has no one than this,
that one lay down his life for his friends. ~ John 15:13

✈ ✈ ✈

In a few minutes, the deputy-leader assumed command, and we dropped back with the group for protection.

Back on the ground, I contacted one of the pilots of the P-51 fighter escort planes and asked him how bad these new German planes were. He said, "Not too bad." He and his partner would split up when one came at the bombers. One would follow it up to keep it in sight and tell his partner where the jet was headed and cut it off. If he missed it, he would follow it to its air base and shoot it down on landing. He said they had learned that the planes only carried enough fuel to fly about 45 minutes, so they had to land.

P-51 Mustang fighter escort plane

A veteran of World War II and the Korean War, North American Aviation's P-51 Mustang was the first U.S. built fighter airplane to push its nose over Europe after the fall of France. Mustangs met and conquered every German plane from the early Junkers to the sleek, twin-jet Messerschmitt 262s.

Although first designed for the British as a medium-altitude fighter, the Mustang excelled in hedgehopping, strafing runs, and long-range escort duty. It made a name for itself by blasting trains, ships, and enemy installations in Western Europe and by devastating Axis defenses before the Allied invasion of Italy.

The Mustang was the first single-engine plane based in Britain to penetrate Germany, first to reach Berlin, first to go with the heavy bombers over the Ploiesti oil fields in Romania, and first to make a major-scale, all-fighter sweep specifically to hunt down the dwindling Luftwaffe.

One of the highest honors accorded to the Mustang was its rating in 1944 by the Truman Senate War Investigating Committee as "the most aerodynamically perfect pursuit plane in existence."

The North American prototype, NA-73X, was first flown on 25 October 1940. At least eight versions of the Mustang were produced.

~ https://www.boeing.com/history/products/p-51-mustang.page

The Russians

On March 31, 1945, we went out on a mission to bomb the Brabag plant northeast of Zeitz, Germany.

Brabag was a German firm, planned in 1933 and operating from 1934 until 1945, that distilled synthetic aviation fuel, diesel fuel, gasoline, lubricants, and paraffin wax from lignite. It was an industrial cartel firm closely supervised by the Nazi regime. While it operated, it produced commodities vital to the German military forces before and during World War II. After substantial damage from strategic bombing, the firm and its remaining assets were dissolved at the end of the war.

~ https://en.wikipedia.org/wiki/Brabag

I was behind and to the left of a B-17 piloted by 1st Lt. A.G. Larsen. His copilot was 1st Lt. Thomas O'Neil, who bunked next to me. As I got to know O'Neil, I discovered that he liked to go to extremes. For example, he went to London and had a pair of sheepskin boots made with a dagger sheath on one of the boots so he could carry a dagger on missions. He always carried two shoulder pistols and a pistol on his side. The only reason we carried pistols was to protect ourselves from the German civilians or the SS youth groups on the ground if we had to bail out. They didn't hesitate to hang American soldiers if they had to parachute out over enemy territory.

1st Lt. Thomas E. O'Neil
~ https://100thbg.com/
(Photo Gallery)

One time we had started to taxi out for a mission, and the commander's car pulled onto the flight line with its red light on and stopped the plane that O'Neil was copiloting. The base commander's driver got out of the car with a .30 caliber carbine, took it to O'Neil, and made him sign for it. We found out later that the base commander was trying to show O'Neil how foolish it was to carry so many guns. If you had to bail out, all the guns on the outside of your clothes would be jerked off.

That March 31, 1945, we went on to complete the mission to Germany, each bomber dropping bombs over the Brabag plant northeast of Zeitz. On the way back to Thorpe Abbotts Air Field, we were flying along in formation when a burst of flak knocked the number three engine off Larsen's plane. The engine went down with the propeller still turning near my right wing. Larsen made a turn to the right, and I called him on the radio to ask if everything was all right. He told me he was going to Switzerland. He didn't want to take a chance on the long flight back to England.

We could see the spectacular Swiss Alps in the distance, sun glinting off the white-capped mountains. Then we saw a parachute come out of the back of Larsen's plane, but no one else came out, and we'd lost all contact with the plane. Three weeks later, Larsen's tail gunner showed up at the base. He said he'd bailed out because the plane was full of smoke, and he couldn't get anyone to answer him on the intercom. He thought they'd bailed out and had left him, so he bailed out and landed on a German air base. He became a prisoner of war, and, when he was interrogated by the Germans, he was informed that Larsen's plane had crashed and all were dead. His captors showed him the crews' dog tags and identifications. The German officer in charge showed him the pilot's wedding ring. The tail gunner asked if he could have the ring so he could return it to Larsen's wife, and the officer gave it to him. Not too long after he was taken prisoner, Russian troops overran the prison, then American troops arrived, and he was flown back to England.

A few days later, another pilot friend, whose cot was near mine, didn't come back from a mission. Every position in the plane was vulnerable; there were no foxholes in the sky. A bomber crewman went about his work without a quiver of conscience, convinced he was fighting for a noble cause. He killed in order not to be killed.

Passes to London and Downtime

We received passes to go to London about four different times, and I was able to visit many of the sights. London is located about 100 miles southwest of Thorpe Abbotts by train. One thing I noticed was every time the train stopped and new passengers boarded their accents changed. Sometimes, I couldn't understand them, but they were nice to anyone in uniform.

On one particular visit to London, several of us decided to go to the beach and sun bathe and swim in the ocean. There were only about six people on the beach, and it was so cold we couldn't stay in the water long, and this was during June. I tried to drink that English beer, but I could never drink more than a cup full. It was too bitter.

During my downtime on base, I never went to the officers' club. Many nights, I would walk over to the flight line, and they would let me tinker with the lathe. I made things like letter openers, and, other times, I'd mount bullets on plastic bases.

The plastics industry came of age during the Second World War. Copper, aluminum, steel, and zinc all became precious metals allocated for military use. Desperate fabricators, who had never thought of plastic as a manufacturing material, began to reconsider. Cellulosic, acrylic, nylon, and especially phenolic and polyethylene became valuable materials. Production was increased. Material manufacturers, machine builders, mold makers, and processors all prospered. That was a terrible war that changed the whole world, but it was the coming of age of the plastics industry.

Plastics are produced from natural gas, feedstocks derived from natural gas processing, and feedstocks derived from crude oil refining.

~ https:// https://www.plasticstoday.com/business/design-world-war-ii-plastics-and-npe

~ https://www.eia.gov/tools/faqs/faq.php?id=34&t=6#:~:text=Although%20crude%20oil%20is%20a,derived%20from%20crude%20oil%20refining

Care packages from home meant the world to everyone at the base. When someone received something special from home, like cookies, they'd share it. V-mail to and from home was one page only. If you wrote small enough, you could write a lot without saying anything about what you were doing or where you were located, for security reasons.

Family members mailed their letters to an APO address located in either New York or San Francisco. I always wrote two letters every few weeks, one to Evelyn and one to my folks, letting them know that I was fine, that I missed them, and that I loved them. They'd always write back, telling me the same thing. It really didn't matter what they said, as long as they sent me a letter. It reminded me what I was fighting for—home, family, freedom.

We only bathed about once a week, if we were lucky. The boiler was heated by coal, and we received a limited amount of coal per week. I took a lot of cold showers. The heaters in our barracks were also coal-fired, again, with a limited amount per week, so someone rigged up a barrel with an oil-and-gasoline mix and piped it to the stove with unlimited fuel. But we had to be careful lighting it, because sometimes it would light with a bang and blow black smoke all over the room.

We were able to get some of the local women to do our laundry. I lived in my long handles and heavy socks. At 30,000 feet, it was 50 degrees below zero. On one flight, my feet got so cold, I had to pull off my boots and rub my feet several times to ward off frostbite. We encountered ice buildup on the windows and carried lighters to melt a hole big enough to see through. Face sweat crystalized into ice pallets. We massaged our oxygen mask intake hoses to breakup any ice that formed from moisture in the breath. Anoxia could occur quickly if tube blockage occurred. When we encountered flak, we put on our flak suits and our steel helmets. We looked like some of the people in today's *Star Wars* movies.

Our flights from England to our bombing targets in Germany were about three hours long (one way), but, on April 7, 1945, aboard *E-Z Goin'*, our flight from Germany back to England would take five, long, hair-raising, energy-draining hours to return to Thorpe Abbotts Air Base.

338514 349th XR-J *E-Z Goin'* at her hardstand prior to 7 April 1945
~ https://100thbg.com/ (Photo Gallery)

Chapter 11

Above all, I shall see to it that the enemy
will not be able to drop any bombs.
~ Hermann Goering, German Air Force Minister.

Rammed at 15,000 Feet (April 7, 1945)

Daring and Desperate Plan

In January 1945, Hitler approved a daring and desperate plan proposed by *Oberst* (Group Captain) Hans-Joachim "Hajo" Hermann. *Reichsmarschall* Hermann Goering agreed that convincing young German pilots to crash their Me-109s into the American bombers would terrorize the crews and force them to stop the bombings. Their plan was implemented on March 8, 1945.

✈ ✈ ✈

The following excerpt is from *Piloto: Migrant Worker To Jet Pilot,* © 2007 (79, 80) by Lt. Col. Henry Cervantes, USAF (Ret.) and my former copilot "Hank." It is quoted here with his permission.

"More than 2,000 German fliers volunteered for the undisclosed mission. Most were recent graduates from flying schools. The best and most experienced pilots, however, were ruled out for they were needed alive.

"The battle plan called for the stripped-down Me-109s to climb to 36,000 feet while, simultaneously, the Me-262s were to stay low and decoy the American fighters away from the bombers. This would free the Elbe pilots to dive down and crash into the unsuspecting bombers.

"At the final stages of preparation, the Germans found that rather than a shortage of volunteers, the overriding problem was a lack of aircraft and fuel. Combat losses together with operational and mechanical problems had whittled down the number of available propeller-driven fighters to no more than 200. In desperation and possibly against their better judgment, they forged ahead with the plan anyway.

"On 6 April 1945, Eighth Air Force Headquarters sent out operational plans for the following day. The orders specified a maximum effort (M.E.) against sixteen targets in northern Germany. Of the Eighth's forty bomb groups, only two would stand-down and of the fourteen fighter groups, one would stay home. (At staff level, such missions were called M.E.'s. Down in the trenches, tongue-in-cheek, they were 'E.G.'s'—everybody goes, including the colonels.)"

Luftwaffe ground crew ("black men") positioning a Bf 109 G-6 equipped with the Rüstsatz VI underwing gondola cannon kit. Note the slats on the leading edge of the port wing. JG 2, France, late 1943.
~ https://en.wikipedia.org/wiki/Messerschmitt_Bf_109#/media/File:Bundesarchiv_Bild_101I-487-3066-04,_Flugzeug_Messerschmitt_Me_109.jpg

The Messerschmitt Bf 109 was a German World War II fighter aircraft that was the backbone of the Luftwaffe's fighter force. It was commonly called the Me-109 most often by Allied aircrew and even amongst the German aces themselves, even though this was not the official German designation.

It was designed by Willy Messerschmitt (hence Me 109) and Robert Lusser, who worked at Bayerische Flugzeugwerke, during the early to mid-1930s. The Bf 109 was the most produced fighter aircraft in history, with a total of 33,984 airframes produced from 1936 up to April 1945.

~ https://en.wikipedia.org/wiki/Messerschmitt_Bf_109

200 *Rammkommando Elbe* Aircraft

On April 7, 1945, our assigned target was to bomb an underground oil storage facility near the German town of Büchen, approximately 66 miles southeast of Frankfurt. The 1,300 bombers, protected by 850 fighters, were directed to fly the mission at exceptionally low altitudes ranging from 14,000 to 21,500 feet. Take-off was scheduled for 0630, assembling altitude at 8,000 feet and flight altitude at 15,200 feet. Once we reached our target and dropped our bombs, we were to climb to 21,000 feet. The estimated time of arrival back at the base for the first squadron would be 1610. But not that day.

Take-off was delayed until 1030 for all bombers and fighters because of heavy fog—zero-zero ceiling and visibility over most of England. And for our nine-man crew, flying *E-Z Goin'* on our 25th mission, it was going to be a very long day. I've included an excerpt from Hank's book, detailing what occurred.

✈ ✈ ✈

The following excerpt is from *Piloto: Migrant Worker To Jet Pilot,* © 2007 (81, 83-89) by Lt. Col. Henry Cervantes, USAF (Ret.) and my former copilot "Hank." It is quoted here with his permission. Occasional remarks from me are noted in brackets.

"At 1130, Luftwaffe air controllers in Central Germany alerted all fighter units that multiple spearheads of American bombers were crossing the channel. Green flares arched high and the last remnants of the German

Air Force including 50 Me-262s and possibly 200 *Rammkommando Elbe* aircraft began their takeoffs.

"Aboard *E-Z Goin',* nearing the Dümmer Lake area [located in the northwestern part of Germany and about 45 minutes from our target] at 1245, we began hearing groups ahead calling for fighter support and all thoughts of a 'milk run' quickly disappeared.

The **Focke-Wulf FW 190** *Würger* (English: Shrike) is a German single-seat, single-engine fighter aircraft designed by Kurt Tank in the late 1930s and widely used during World War II. Along with its well-known counterpart, the Messerschmitt Bf 109, the FW 190 became the backbone of the Luftwaffe's Jagdwaffe (Fighter Force).
~ https://en.wikipedia.org/wiki/Focke-Wulf_FW_190

"Suddenly, an FW-190 sliced in front of us firing at Lieutenant William Howard's B-17 forward and left of us. Immediately, bright orange flames engulfed the number three engine and wheel-well. Howard salvoed his bombs and shut down the engine. His navigator, Lieutenant D.R. Jones, was Tony's [Navigator, 2nd Lt. Antonio Picone] friend; and as they fell back, Tony shouted, 'Hey look that plane's on fire. Oh hell, that's Jonesy's plane. Let's drop back and protect them.'

"'Can't do that, Tony,' Joe said. Silence. Their copilot, Lieutenant Genaro Delgado, was my friend, and as they began a 180-degree turn trailing thick black smoke, I [Hank] thought, well, there goes half of the 100th's supply of Mexican pilots. (While in the service, Gerry was the only Latino military pilot I ever met. I am not saying there weren't more, I just didn't meet any.)

"Howard leveled off and the crew came tumbling out like sacks of dirty GI laundry. Later, we learned that three men died with the plane. Howard, Delgado, and Jones survived, although Jones got his front teeth knocked out by angry [German] civilians.

"The battle continued and the intercom was alive with gunners calling out enemy planes to each other. Gerling [Tail Gunner, S/Sgt. Paul Gerling] shouted, 'Here comes one from five o'clock high!' I [Hank] looked to my right just as a Me-109 swooshed by us so close that we bounced from the shock wave. Inexplicably, the pilot hadn't shot at us nor was he at his gun-sight aiming at someone below—he was looking at me. We stared at each other for a fleeting moment, and then he was gone. He rammed Lieutenant Arthur Calder's *Candy's Dandy* in the squadron below, the two planes exploded and everyone died.

Arthur R. Calder, 418th P, New York, KIA 7 April 1945 Büchan, Arthur R. Calder Crew
~ https://100thbg.com/ (Photo Gallery)

"Elsewhere, a Me-109 pilot crashed his right wing into the left side of a B-17 in the 490th Bomb Group. The fighter twisted under the fuselage, cartwheeled across the bomber's underbelly damaging the number three and four engines then fell away. The bomber turned back and landed on a friendly fighter strip. In the 452nd Bomb Group, two B-17s were rammed by FW-190s and all four went down. Classmate Jim Simouse was the copilot of one of them. In the 389th, a B-24 group, a Me-109 crashed into the nose of the lead bomber. The decapitated Liberator veered left into the right wing of the deputy leader's plane and all three went down. FW-190s also rammed two B-17s in the 388th, and the 550th lost *Van's Valiants* to a rammer, as did the 493rd when *Lady Helene* was rammed and crashed. In the 389th, *The Sky Scorpion* met the same fate. While over in the 487th, a B-24 lost its starboard fin and rudder to a Me-109 but was able to land on the continent along with other rammed planes from the 490th and 487th Bomb Groups. Twelve other bombers, including classmate Lieutenant Walter Center's *Happy Warrior*, also went down for one reason or another. Throughout the battle, our more experienced fighter pilots were having a field day with the unskilled Germans.

Caaarraash!

"*Caaarraash! E-Z Goin's* nose yawed left, we skidded right, and the fuselage shuddered like a dog shaking water off itself. Instinctively, Joe and I [Hank] kicked hard right rudder, both pedals disappeared under the instrument panel then returned and dangled uselessly. The time was 1323.

"The control columns were violently jerking back and forth, the number one engine was streaming smoke, and all the radios including the intercom were out. Lacking an intercom, we had no way to determine the crew's plight or to assess the damage. *E-Z Goin'* seemed to still want to fly, though, so we stabilized the rocking, rolling motion with the ailerons [on the wings] and hung on.

"Five minutes later we arrived over the target [Büchen]. Ralph [Togglier/Nose Gunner, S/Sgt. Ralph Spada] called 'Bombs away' [flipped a switch in the Plexiglas nose compartment of the plane to release the bombs from the bomb bay compartment], and the nose lurched up sharply as the bombs tumbled out. Joe rolled the elevator trim wheel forward to add nose-down trim but the wheel spun uselessly.

"We pushed with all our strength on the control columns but could not exert sufficient force to stop us from rapidly climbing toward another B-17 above us. At the last possible moment, Joe retarded the throttles and *E-Z Goin'* shuddered into a stall. The two B-17s slid by close enough to swap paint. By trial and error, we found that at 105-110 miles an hour, just above the stall speed at that altitude, we could maintain level flight. The number one engine appeared ready to catch fire so we shut it down as strung-out remnants of the 100th [Bomb Group] disappeared into the haze and we remained behind to wallow through the sky alone.

"The attacks finally tapered off and Dude [Top Turret Gunner/Engineer, T/Sgt. William "Dude" E. Dudecz] toured the ship to assess our condition. He reported back, 'Everyone's OK. Paul [Tail Gunner, S/Sgt. Paul Gerling] says that a Me-109 crashed into us. There's two big slashes in the fuselage aft of the left gunner's window and the flight control cables and electric wire bundles are cut there too. What's left of the tail's flapping up and down so hard that it looks like the fuselage might break in two. The left elevator and the top half of the rudder are gone and there are bullet holes in the left side of the nose. We think a gunner in another B-17 was tracking the 109 that crashed into us and shot out our number one engine and the master radio control box. That's why the radios are dead. Tony was reaching down to pick up a map or they would have gotten him, too.'

Under attack – enemy aircraft in pursuit at 6 o'clock high.
~ https://100thbg.com/ (Photo Gallery)

"On a B-17, the tips of the horizontal stabilizers are visible from the pilots' windows and I looked back to see what was causing the control wheels to jerk back and forth so forcefully.

"'Joe,' I said, 'Dude's right. The tail's really bobbing up and down on my side. What's yours doing?'

"Joe checked his and asked, 'Are you sure we're supposed to be able to see the tail from here?'

"'Yeah, I'm sure.'

"'I don't have one.' [Joe: I couldn't see the left horizontal stabilizer/elevator of the tail section, which I should have been able to see. It was totally gone along with the top half of the tail.]

"Dude tapped me [Hank] on the shoulder and asked, 'Do you want to come back and take a closer look at the damage?'

"'No, Dude, I'm needed here. (Truthfully, I was afraid of what I might see.) How's Paul doing? Is he still in the tail?'

"'No, I ordered him out of there. He says that when parts from our plane went flying back, they knocked off the left horizontal stabilizer on another B-17 behind us. They're back there somewhere.'

"We later learned that Captain [2nd Lt.] Joe King also nursed his damaged B-17 home to a safe landing.

"Two P-51s came by. The pilots bracketed us and tried to establish radio contact. I [Hank] signaled that our radios were dead so they looked us over, shook their heads hard, gave us a 'thumbs up,' and headed home. To us, their departure indicated that we were no longer vulnerable to enemy attacks. The crew jettisoned [Joe's orders] everything possible but the emergency equipment and with that, the airspeed increased by an encouraging blip or two on the dial. We breathed a bit easier.

Decision Time

"An hour later, the coastline came into view and it was decision time again. Should we attempt a landing on one of the many abandoned fighter airstrips below us? If so, we risked landing on a damaged runway or having the tail break off on touchdown with no medical help available. On the other hand, a decision to continue on to England required that *E-Z Goin'* hold together long enough to cross 150 miles of the North Sea. Further, we would then have to let down through the overcast without radio communications, locate an airfield, and land on instruments. We decided to chance it. I [Hank] dialed in the Thorpe Abbotts frequency on the Instrument Landing System (ILS).

"The system uses two fixed radio beams to guide a plane to a landing; one beam provides lateral guidance and the other establishes a glide path to the runway. The cockpit display on this instrument consists of two crossed needles. Stray off course left or right and the error is revealed in the movement of a vertical needle. Stray above or below the glide slope and a horizontal needle provides that indication.

"Surprisingly, the ILS seemed to be operating properly. With the radios inoperative, however, we could not verify what station, if any, it had locked on to. We gambled that the instrument had acquired our home instrument landing system and would guide us there.

"We began a long, slow descent into the clouds. Two hours later, as we neared the ground but still had not broken out, we knew that the morning fog had returned. I had a troubled feeling that we were about to die.

"We broke out at 700 feet above the ground with a mile visibility and our home runway directly ahead. It was as if God had finally decided that we had been tested enough and intended to let us live—for now. As we made a sweeping turn into a long final approach to the runway, Norman Larsen [Radio Operator/Gunner, Sgt. Norman Larsen] began firing red-red flares and Joe signaled, 'wheels down.' I flipped the landing gear switch but nothing happened; the landing gear motor was inoperative. Quickly, Dude scurried back to the bomb bay where he manually cranked the gear down with the emergency system. The green indicator light came on.

"We were nearing touchdown when another B-17 also firing red flares cut in front of us to land. [We learned later that he had wounded aboard.] We had no alternative but to go around. That, however, is quite impossible to do on only three engines, with the wheels down, and no rudder control. Dude laboriously cranked the gear up. Flight procedures called for us to waggle the wings at the control tower to indicate 'Radio Failure.' We disregarded the rule for fear the lateral air pressures might further damage the tail—external damage would have to communicate the caliber of our problem. As we staggered over nearby villages at treetop level, traffic stopped and people scrambled out of stores and cars to point at us. Given the number of damaged B-17s most of them had probably seen, the attention seemed a dubious honor.

"We returned to the final approach. Dude cranked the gear down again, the crew assumed their crash-landing positions, and Joe brought us in for a perfect two-point landing. I held my breath as we gently lowered the tail wheel to the runway. *E-Z Goin'* screeched, grated, and groaned like a giant beer can being scrunched on a sidewalk, but she held together. A plume of emergency vehicles trailed us to our hardstand [the concrete circular pad on which a bomber is parked off the runway] where we shut down the remaining three engines. Five hours had elapsed since the collision but no one cheered, embraced, or even shook Joe's hand. Perhaps we would have shown greater appreciation had we realized that the extraordinary feat of airmanship which Joe Martin performed that day has been rarely if ever equaled by a pilot with 800 hours of total flying time. But at that age, everyone thinks he is going to live forever and that death only claims others, not him.

Nine Very Lucky Airmen

"When I was in flight school, our theory of flight instructors explained

> *LAURENCE J. LAZZARI CREW HISTORY*
> *Written for the most part by G. G. Greenwood*
>
> *23. (Z96) Buchen, Germany. 1327 Hours. 4/7/45. 14.880 feet. 6ea 1000 pound RDX's. 2 bursts of accurate flak. We were under fighter attack for 33 minutes; ME-109's. Two planes and crews were lost today. We saw one of them shot down. The picture of 1317 43-33514 on the cover of CENTURY BOMBERS, which had a ME-109 fly through its tail, was piloted by Joe Martin and copiloted by Henry Cervantes. Classmates at Rapid City. We saw the 100th gunners shoot down the ME-109, in fact, it was so close that we saw the ME-109 pilot slump over his stick as our gunner's bullets hit him. CENTURY BOMBERS page 196 does not give Martin and Cervantes credit for bringing this plane home. As the fighter collided with Martin's tail, his B-17's nose went up in a 45 degree angle, and I thought that he was going to spin in, but he got the plane stabilized and brought her home. I hope that Martin got the DFC for that performance. We heard later that Martin made the best landing of the day even though he had very little rudder and elevator control. He had to, for if he had not, he probably would not have made it. Mission time was 8+45 hours.*
>
> *~ https://100thbg.com/index.php?option=com_content&view=article&id=247:lazzari-crew-history&catid=25:group-history&Itemid=581*

the rule in physics that governs why an airplane must have a tail to fly. I didn't question their wisdom then. But less than a year later, on 7 April 1945, God made an exception to the rule for nine very lucky airmen.

"During debriefing, several pilots commented on the extraordinary aggressiveness of the German fighter attacks. The debriefers, however, pooh-poohed our remarks and refused to give them any validity. During that last air battle of the war, escort fighter units collectively claimed 90 victories while bomber unit gunners made claims of 41 destroyed and 26 probables. The 100th's gunners claimed eight kills. I questioned the marksmen but none asked to be credited with shooting up our B-17.

"Exaggerations about our flight persist to this day. One of the more popular tales alleges that, 'Because the flight control cables to the tail were severed, the pilots made it back to Thorpe Abbotts with the help of the crew, who moved to the rear of the plane to raise the nose and to the front to lower it.' Whenever asked to confirm the story, I facetiously reply, 'Certainly it's true. You should have seen me directing traffic when we came in to land then had to go around.' They forgot that our right [horizontal] elevator remained operational throughout the flight."

Standing L-R: S/Sgt. Ralph E. Spada, togglier(bombardier)/nose guns; S/Sgt. Matthew Schipper, waist guns; Sgt. Alfred S. Collins, ball turret guns; S/Sgt. Paul R. Gerling, tail guns; 1st Lt. Joe Carl Martin, Jr., pilot; 2nd Lt. Antonio Picone, navigator; Warrant Officer Hank Cervantes, copilot. Kneeling (L-R): T/Sgt. William Dudecz, top turret guns/engineer; Sgt. Norman E. Larsen, radio operator/waist guns. ~ https://100thbg.com/ (Photo Gallery)

✈ ✈ ✈

Chapter 12

Do not be afraid. Stand firm and you will see the deliverance the Lord will bring you today. ~ Exodus 14:13 (NIV)

Aftermath (April 7, 1945)

Flying in Close Formation

In a B-17, prop wash, also known as wake turbulence, caused violent buffeting and loss of control, which you don't want to happen while flying in close formation. Even though we were staggered both horizontally and vertically, we flew in tight formations to provide greater protection against German fighter attacks.

At the end of two or three hours at the controls, your arms, legs, and back are stiff with pain. At high altitude, your feet are going numb from the cold. The goggles over your eyes fog up from the heat of your skin, while you're trying to read gauges and scan the sky for enemy flak and enemy jets that seem to come out of nowhere, fast. The oxygen mask feels like a choking hand over your face, and the throat mike scrubs against the smallest shaving wound you might have. The roar of the four engines is deafening, which is why your flight helmet has earphones so you can hear your crew and the pilots from the other planes flying off your left and right wings as well as above and below you.

Combat Wing: Below and angled view.
~ https://100thbg.com/ (Photo Gallery)

Layers of Gear

And let's not forget the layers of gear you're wearing to stay warm in the uninsulated cockpit that's small and crowded with every type of instrument needed to pilot a Flying Fortress. Did I mention the Mae West life jacket in case we had to ditch at sea? We also carried French Francs on us in case our plane crashed so we would have money to help us get back to England. Then there was the .45 caliber automatic pistol tucked into the waist holster on my right side and the harnessed parachute that I sat on in case we had to bail out, *if* I'm able to get to the bomb bay doors in the belly of the ship, after my crew bails out and before the plane crashes or explodes.

While Hank was working in tandem with me, manhandling *E-Z Goin'* to stay in the air, the rest of my crew were at their assigned stations, carrying out their assigned tasks. However, because of the tail damage, my tail gunner took up a position with the waist gunner, manning the second gun. Just so you know, my crew was wearing the same type outfit as I was.

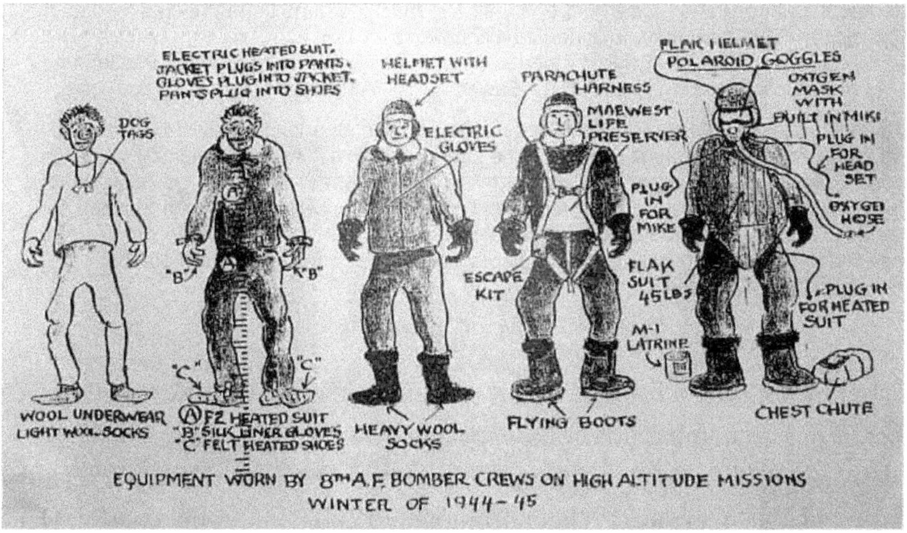

What we wore at minus 50 degrees F. ~ http://evanflys.com/jack_burke

How to Bail Out of the Flying Fortress

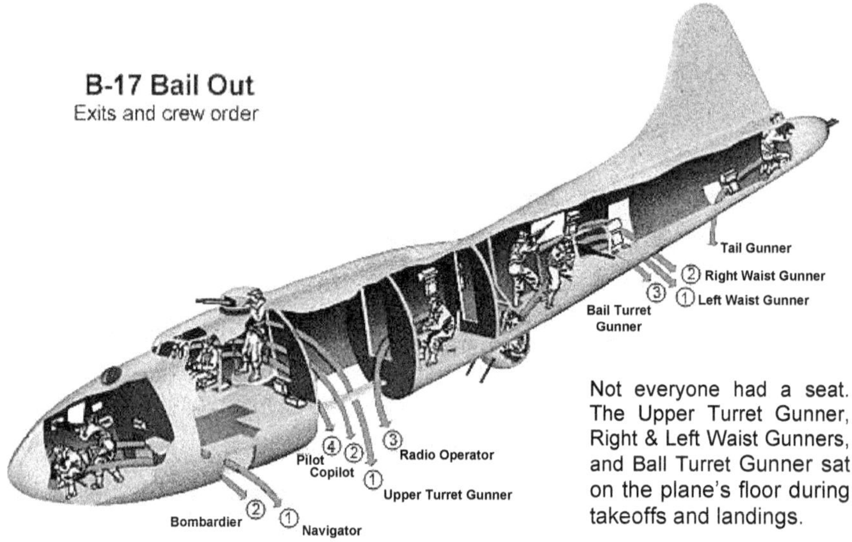

Not everyone had a seat. The Upper Turret Gunner, Right & Left Waist Gunners, and Ball Turret Gunner sat on the plane's floor during takeoffs and landings.

From the crewman's manual for the B-17 showing where each crewman worked and how he bailed out. Notice that four crewmen bail out through the bomb bay. The B-17 was crewed by four officers (two pilots, navigator, and bombardier) and six enlisted men (top turret gunner/crew chief, radioman/gunner, ball turret gunner, two waist gunners, and tail gunner). In the tail position, the gunner sat on a bicycle seat at the base of the fourteen-foot rear stabilizer and rudder and operated two machine guns that protected the tail of the aircraft. This, of course, is under ideal conditions.

~ http://www.in2guitar.com/b-17.html
~ http://www.381st.org/Aircraft/B-17-Basics
~ B-17 Flying Fortress Walkaround "Aluminum Overcast" - YouTube

As a personal FYI, the fuselage, or body of an airplane, is a long hollow tube that holds all the pieces of an airplane together. The interior of a B-17 was exceptionally hollow to reduce weight, consisting of bare bones, rivets, and exposed wires, with no insulation of any kind. You couldn't stand up straight, and you had to be careful when you reached out to steady yourself. A heater was considered nonessential. A B-17 carried only what it needed to fly, communicate, navigate, photograph, shoot bullets, and drop bombs.

~ Joe Carl Martin, Jr.

My Crew

Let me tell you a little bit about the fantastic crew who flew with me on most of our 26 combat missions, especially on April 7, 1945.

Cervantes

My copilot, **Warrant Officer Henry "Hank" Cervantes** (later promoted to 2nd Lt.): As my copilot, Hank was the executive officer—my chief assistant, understudy, and strong right arm. He was familiar with every one of my duties—both as pilot and as airplane commander—and able to take over and act in my place at any time. He was a fully trained, rated pilot just like me. The B-17 is a lot of airplane, more airplane than any one pilot can handle alone over a long period of time. Therefore, a second pilot is necessary to share the duties of flight operation.

My navigator, **2nd Lt. Antonio "Tony" Picone**: As navigator, Tony directed our flights from departure to destination and back. He knew the exact position of our plane at all times. Navigation is the art of determining geographic positions by means of (a) pilotage, (b) dead reckoning, (c) radio, or (d) celestial navigation, or any combination of those four methods. The navigator determines the position of the airplane in relation to the earth, navigating the plane with a high degree of accuracy. He also has a general knowledge of the entire operation of the airplane. He has a .50-caliber machine gun at his station, and he is able to use it skillfully and to service it in emergencies. He is familiar with the oxygen system, knows how to operate the turrets, radio equipment, and fuel transfer system. He knows the location of all fuses and spare fuses, lights and spare lights, affecting navigation. He is familiar with emergency procedures, such as the manual operation of landing gear, bomb bay doors, and flaps, and the proper procedures for crash landings, ditching, bailout, etc.

Picone

Bombardier & Navigator Compartment in nose of B-17.
~ https://farm2.staticflickr.com/1496/26150445002_3a1fa75288_b.jpg

My togglier(bombardier)/nose gunner, **S/Sgt. Ralph Spada**: The bombardier is familiar with the duties of all members of the crew and is able to assist the navigator in case the navigator becomes incapacitated. In addition to dropping bombs, he also has a .50-cal. machine gun at his station. In a B-17G, he also operates the two chin turret .50-cal. machine guns. Accurate and effective bombing is the ultimate purpose of the airplane and crew. Every other function is preparatory to hitting and destroying the target. That's the

Spada

bombardier's job. The success or failure of the mission depends upon what he accomplishes in that short interval of the bombing run.

My radio operator/gunner, **Sgt. Norman Larsen**: There is a lot of radio equipment in a B-17. Training in the various phases of the heavy bomber program is designed to fit each member of the crew for the handling of his job. In addition to being a radio operator, he is also a gunner.

Larsen

During periods of combat, he is required to leave his watch at the radio and take up his gun. He is required to learn photography. Some of the best pictures taken in the Southwest Pacific were taken by radio operators.

There's a great deal more equipment in the radio compartment than what is shown in these photos, including a large camera for taking aerial photos.
~ https://www.ohio.edu/people/mcfadden/img/b-17_radio_position.jpg

Collins

My gunners:

- Ball turret gunner, **Cpl. Alfred S. Collins**
- Tail gunner, **S/Sgt. Paul Gerling**
- Waist gunner, **S/Sgt. Matthew "Matt" Schipper**

Gerling

Schipper

Gunners belong to one of two distinct categories: power turret gunners and flexible gunners. The power turret gunners require many mental and physical qualities similar to what we know as inherent flying ability, since the operation of the power turret and gunsight are much like that of airplane flight operation. While the flexible gunners do not require the same delicate touch as the turret gunner, they have a fine sense of timing and are familiar with the rudiments of exterior ballistics. All gunners are familiar with the coverage area of all gun positions and are prepared to bring the proper gun to bear as the conditions may warrant. They are experts in aircraft identification. They are thoroughly familiar with the aircraft machine guns. They know how to maintain the guns, how to clear jams and stoppages, and how to harmonize the sights with the guns.

Frank Reese Mays (aka "Junior"): Ball Turret Gunner on the "WAR HORSE" – 35+ Combat Missions in the Ball Turret ~ http://iwvpa.net/jarrellr/index.php

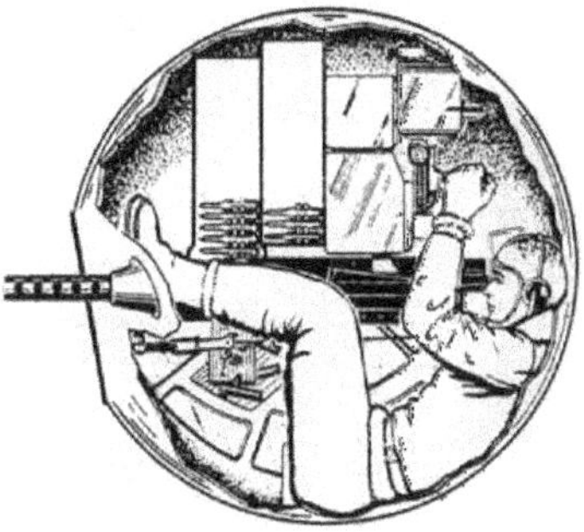

~ https://s-media-cache-ak0.pinimg.com/originals/07/12/1c/07121c6d2ba46d6ce9f230a27ac69b41.gif

"A ball turret was a Plexiglas sphere set into the belly of a B-17 or B-24 bomber and inhabited by two.50 caliber machine-guns and one man—a short, small man. When this gunner tracked with his machine guns at a fighter attacking his bomber from below, he revolved the turret." (Jarrell's notes)

My top turret gunner/engineer, **T/Sgt. William "Dude" E. Dudecz**: To be a qualified combat engineer, a man must know his airplane, his engines, and his armament equipment thoroughly. The lives of the entire crew, the safety of the equipment, and the success of the mission depend upon it squarely. He works closely with the copilot, checking engine operation, fuel consumption, and the operation of all equipment. He is able to work with the bombardier and knows how to cock, lock, and load the bomb racks. He knows how to strip, clean, and re-assemble the guns. He has a general knowledge of radio equipment and is able to assist in tuning transmitters and receivers. The engineer is the chief source of information concerning the airplane. He knows more about the equipment than any other crewmember, including the pilot.

Dudecz

Top Turret Gunner
~ http://www.twinbeech.com/images/Aircraft/armament/gunnery/turrets/sperry/A-1forsale/1_09_3.jpg

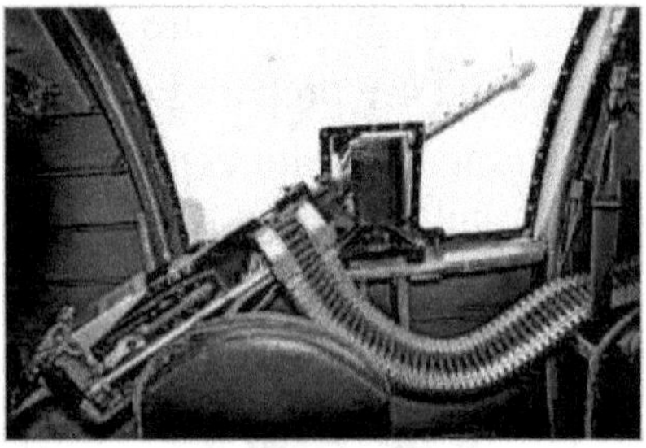

Bombers had single .50 caliber free-flexible waist guns on each side. This one is in a B-17G.
~ http://weaponsman.com/?p=10038

Just Fly The Plane

When the initial crash happened, I didn't know right away how badly we'd been hit, but I put into action everything I'd been taught. You learn in flight school to keep it trim and "just fly the plane." As a pilot, you act, and you act fast. The lives of your crew depend on it. Sometimes, you only have seconds to make a decision and hope it's the right one. A sudden panic can take over, and you can forget your training when you see certain death in front of you.

When the Me-109 hit *E-Z Goin'*s tail, her nose yawed left, suddenly pointing us skyward at a steep angle. We skidded right, the whole fuselage shaking violently. We were headed right for the Lead Plane above us. The rudder pedals at our feet disappeared beneath the instrument panel. The control columns would not respond to our efforts to keep from climbing higher. I rolled the elevator trim wheel forward to add nose-down trim, but the wheel spun uselessly. The number one engine was streaming smoke, and all the electronics like the autopilot, the radios, including the intercom were dead.

Inches separated *E-Z Goin'* from the Lead Plane. My heart was pumping so hard and fast I could feel the pounding in my head. That's when I told the Lord He was the copilot and would He please take over.

Some pilots swear. I pray with my eyes wide open. He doesn't always answer my prayers right away. Sometimes, not at all. This time He did.

Instantly, He reminded me what I'd learned in the Vultee Vibrator—retard the throttles (slow the engine speed), which dropped us into a stall speed so the wings would lose lift and add a lot of drag. We stabilized the rocking, rolling motion with the ailerons on the wings and leveled off just as we approached the target to drop our bombs. My heart settled a bit.

The Lead Plane signaled, "bombs away," and, without the autopilot, I had to hold the plane steady and on course so my Togglier/Nose Gunner, S/Sgt. Ralph Spada, could drop the bombs on the designated target. I knew we would lurch up once he pulled the toggle switch to release the bombs. Normally, once the bombs were dropped, I'd release the autopilot so I'd have control of the plane again. Then we'd automatically ascend as a group to 20,000 feet and out of the direct aim of the flak guns below us. But not that day.

April 7, 1945.
Inflight photo just after being rammed.

We were off the Lead Plane's left wing at the outer edge of the combat box as we dropped our bombs. All the other planes dropped their bombs and quickly gained altitude. We lacked the engine speed to keep up, so we dropped out of formation, drifting off to the left, losing altitude with about five hours of fuel left, and finding ourselves alone and vulnerable to additional attacks. Flak exploded all around us as we turned back toward the coast and the North Sea. Two P-51s escorted us a short ways while keeping the German jets and Me-109s from trying to take us down.

As we approached 150 miles of open water on three engines with a damaged tail that felt like it would break off any minute, I knew it was going to take every bit of our remaining fuel to get us back to Thorpe Abbotts. It was going to be close because planes burn more fuel at lower altitudes. *E-Z Goin'* had responded to everything we'd asked her to do, so I gave the order to lighten our load, throwing out everything we didn't need, including the guns and ammo, to keep from losing any more altitude. We maintained our thrust at 105-110 mph, just above stall speed, as we continued to lose altitude to 1,000 feet above the ocean waves. My crew expressed their concerns about having to ditch in the sea.

I told them, "I'm not going for a swim today." God had carried us this far. I prayed that He would carry us the rest of the way.

When we finally approached the English coast, the fog was so thick we couldn't see any land mass or lights. We flew on instruments only, with our navigator telling us where we were.

A lot of pilots don't trust their instruments and crash. We trusted our instruments. We trusted that 2nd Lt. Tony Picone knew exactly where we were at all times. I trusted that God had heard my prayers.

As we approached where Thorpe Abbotts Air Base should be, Tony said, "It ought to be right under us." We finally cleared the fog at 700 feet and were right over the base, lining up to land when another B-17, carrying wounded and firing red flares, cut us off. We were forced to circle, struggling to gain some altitude, right over the villages and cottages dotting the area before we could line up again and land.

We were able to maintain level flight all the way back to base and landed with less than 30 minutes of fuel left in our tanks. The normal three-hour return flight from Germany was the longest five hours of my life.

After we landed at Thorpe Abbotts and came to our hardstand, I shut down the three remaining engines. Sitting there for a moment, I gave a quick prayer of thanks then followed my crew out to walk around *E-Z Goin'*, checking out the damage she'd sustained, especially the tail.

We later determined that one of the gunners, possibly from the Lead Plane, fired .50 caliber rounds at the Me-109 that had hit us. Unfortunately, the gunner hit our number one engine and the small box near my feet, which took out all the electronics for the plane. The repair crew found .50 caliber shells lodged in the seat where my navigator sat.

The base commander, Colonel Sutterlin, drove out to meet us at our hardstand and congratulated me for bringing the plane back. I kiddingly said, "All in a day's work." But that's not what I was thinking.

Before each mission, I always said a prayer that the Lord would guide me in the ways that would best honor Him, that He would deliver my crew from harm, and that He would deliver me safely home to my beautiful bride.

As I looked at what was left of the tail and my crew standing around safe and sound, I had no doubt He'd heard my prayers. Not only was God's hand on my shoulder on April 7, 1945, I knew He'd been holding *E-Z Goin'* in the palm of His hand.

COLLISION OVER BUCHEN
100th BOMB GROUP / 349th SQUADRON
E-Z GOIN'

In one of the last air battles with the Luftwaffe on April 7, 1945, E-Z GOIN', a B-17G with the "Bloody 100th" Bomb Group, had a mid-air collision with an ME-109. The flight crew continued on to bomb their target in Buchen, Germany, and returned to make a safe landing at their home base in England.

Lonnie Ortega © 1992
Signed by Henry Cervantes, Norman E. Larsen, Joe C. Martin, and Paul R. Gerling

~ hittps://100thbg.com/ (Photo Gallery)

Chapter 13

Never in the field of human conflict
was so much owed by so many to so few.
~ Winston Churchill

Thank You Boys
(April-May 1945)

Lady Evelyn

The next day, April 8, our commanding officer wanted us to go up again but flying a different B-17. I was ready, but my crew was very apprehensive and worried about going up again so soon. It was finally decided that our crew, along with other crews whose planes had been badly damaged in the Luftwaffe's aerial assault, would have seven days R&R at a castle south of London.

The castle had been set aside by the owners for troops to recover and relax in. The bedrooms had names on the doors and mine had Lady Evelyn, the same as my wife.

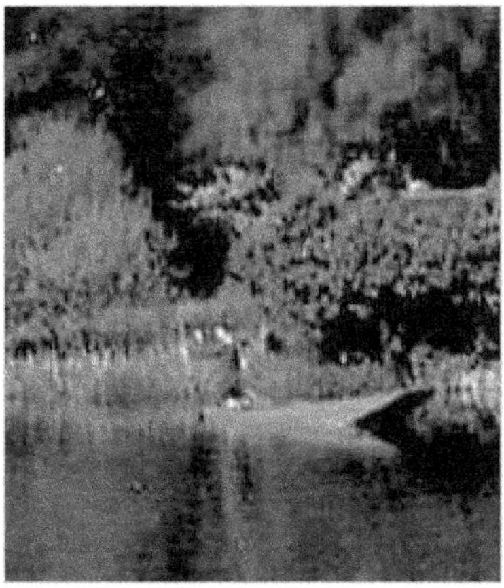

Me in the boat in the middle of the lake on the property.

There was a large family living next door to the castle who took care of everyone's needs, such as cooking, washing, and gardening. The meals were simple, and our hosts were gracious. The front lawn covered at least a half mile down a gentle slope of various colors of roses and green hedges. In spite of the war, everything was immaculate.

I didn't accompany my crew to town. Most of the time, I'd explore the castle and its grounds and enjoy the quiet while fishing in a nearby lake.

While we were gone, *E-Z Goin'* was fitted with a new tail and repairs made to the other battle damage. *E-Z Goin's* crew chief, Master Sergeant Alfred T. Conte, and his team of experts completed the job in seven days.

1. Master Sergeant Alfred T. Conte, *E-Z Goin's* crew chief.
2. Crew working on the tail section.
3. Discarded tail section.

~ https://100thbg.com/ (Photo Gallery)

Returned to Flying Status

Upon our return to Thorpe Abbotts, our crew was returned to flying status, and, on April 20, 1945, we flew *E-Z Goin'* on our 26th mission—our last combat mission—to Oranienburg. The 100th Bomb Group took off at 0600 and headed for Oranienburg, where at 1015 and from 22,500 feet, twenty-nine of its planes released ten 500-pound bombs on the rail marshalling yards with good results. *E-Z Goin'* flew like a wounded duck, but it was great to have her back.

The following morning we were briefed on bombing an airport near Munich, but the mission was scrubbed before take-off. Then on April 23, we prepared to hit the Büchen railroad station, but, again, the flight was canceled. It suddenly occurred to everyone that there was no place left to bomb.

For the 100th Bomb Group, the war was over. Between June 12, 1943, and April 20, 1945, the group had flown 306 combat missions with 351 B-17s and credited with 8,630 sorties—attacks made by troops coming from a position of defense. Total bomb tonnage dropped was 19,257. There were 184 Missing Air Crew reports (9- or 10-man crews). Of those missing, 768 men were classified as killed in action or missing in action. Of the aircrews forced down over enemy territory and survived the crash, 939 men were captured and became POWs.

The group lost a total of 1,772 crewmembers for all causes. The number of planes that went down due to enemy action was 229. Of those, 61 were salvaged at the field, and 25 were returned to the States, with *E-Z Goin'* among them.

Our nine-member crew flew 228 combat hours on 26 missions. During our combat flights (February 19 to April 20, 1945), the 100th lost fourteen B-17s, and the group's gunners shot down fifteen enemy fighters including several jets.

On April 30, 1945, Nazi Leader Adolf Hitler committed suicide during the Battle of Berlin, April 16 to May 2, 1945 (invasion of Russian Army).

The 100th Bombardment Group (Heavy) was an Eighth Air Force B-17 Flying Fortress unit in England, stationed at RAF Thorpe Abbotts. Flying over 300 combat missions, the group earned two Distinguished Unit Citations (Regensburg, 17 August 1943; Berlin, 4/6/8 March 1944). The group suffered tremendous losses in combat, with 177 Aircraft MIA, flying its last mission on 20 April 1945.

Today's 100th Air Refueling Wing (100th ARW) is a United States Air Force unit assigned to the Third Air Force, United States Air Forces in Europe - Air Forces Africa. It is stationed at RAF Mildenhall, England. It is also the host wing at RAF Mildenhall.

The 100th ARW is the only permanent U.S. air-refueling wing in the European theater. One of the wing's honors is that it is the only modern USAF operational wing allowed to display on its assigned aircraft the tail code (Square-D) of its World War II predecessor.

~ https://en.wikipedia.org/wiki/100th_Air_Refueling_Wing

Operation Manna

✈ ✈ ✈

The following excerpt is from *Piloto: Migrant Worker To Jet Pilot,* © 2007 (97-98) by Lt. Col. Henry Cervantes, USAF (Ret.) and my former copilot "Hank." It is quoted here with his permission. Occasional remarks from me are noted in brackets.

"The ground war continued [in spite of Hitler's suicide]. [General] Eisenhower [Supreme Allied Commander] had bypassed strong German forces in the Netherlands for fear they might blow up the dikes in retribution for a ground attack. Dutch civilians, however, were starving to death at a rate approaching 1,000 a day, and, after some maneuvering, the German commander allowed us to make food drops to provide a measure of relief. The agreement required that we stay under 500 feet, remain within strictly mandated corridors, and not carry gunners aboard. No one felt better when the briefer added, 'Anyone fired upon will receive credit for a combat mission.'

"The modified bomb bays were loaded with boxes of ten-in-one rations, and on May 3rd we flew on the first of several 'Operation Manna' missions. We went in at wave-top level, hopped over the dikes, and skimmed by telephone poles in an effort to stay as low as possible. German flak batteries were everywhere, and we kept a wary eye on the gunners who squinted at us like duck hunters waiting for the season to open.

Official 8th Air Force photo of a 390th BG, 13th Combat Wing ship during the Chowhound Mission [aka Operation Manna]. ~ https://100thbg.com/ (Photo Gallery)

Manna from the heavens, the food parcels dropped from the B-17s of the 3rd Air Division. ~ https://100thbg.com/ (Photo Gallery)

THANK YOU BOYS spelled out in a field showing the gratitude of the Dutch people. Photo from the 490th BG on the 5-4-45 food drop. Photo courtesy of Eric Swain, 490th BG Historian ~ https://100thbg.com/ (Photo Gallery)

Lead crew drop photo showing target of a white cross and the food cartons falling around it. (Photo courtesy of Rich Rock) ~ https://100th bg.com/ (Photo Gallery)

Dutch people harvesting the 10 in 1 food cartons while more manna falls from the skies. ~ https://100thbg.com/ (Photo Gallery)

"Early May is tulip time in Holland and despite the ugly scars of war, carpets of blazing colors dotted the countryside. Joyful women and children were everywhere. Some waved American and Dutch flags at us while others pointed to messages in open fields that read, 'Thank You Boys,' and the like. Near Amsterdam, we 'bombed' an open field centered with a white cross that appeared to be fashioned from bed sheets. Below us, it was a free-for-all as civilians with German soldiers among them could be seen scrambling for boxes as even more of the 50-pound missiles showered down.

> *The daughter of a Dutch baroness and a British father, who left the family when [future actress] Audrey Hepburn was 6, the ballet student barely survived the German occupation of Holland, which began when she was 11. She had to hide in the basement for days without food. It was the winter of hunger [1944-45], when the Nazis starved hundreds of thousands of people in Holland in retaliation for their support of the Allies.*
>
> *~ Robert Wolders, Audrey Hepburn's partner from 1980 until her death in 1993; excerpt from article in "People" magazine, August 28, 2017 (46)*

"On May 5th, we repeated our performance over Bergen and were again treated to the heartwarming sight of mothers hugging their kids as they pointed at the big grins on our faces.

"The war [in Europe] ended on May 8th, and, the following day our adjutant, Major Horace Varian, swore me [Hank] in as a second lieutenant."

✈ ✈ ✈

Germany's surrender was authorized by Hitler's successor, *Reichspräsident* Karl Dönitz. The administration headed by Dönitz was known as the Flensburg Government. The act of military surrender was signed on May 7, 1945, in Reims, France, and on May 8, 1945, in Berlin, Germany.

Victory in Europe Day, generally known as **V-E Day**, was the public holiday celebrated on May 8, 1945, to mark the formal acceptance by the Allies of World War II of Nazi Germany's unconditional surrender of its armed forces. It thus marked the end of World War II in Europe.

Ferrying POWs

We flew to several places to bring prisoners of war back to France. The bomb bays had been modified with wood pallets so our guests would have a place to sit. On one trip on May 20, 1945, we had to land in Linz, Austria, where we loaded up with French officers, soldiers, and civilians. They'd been sprayed with a bug killer before loading, and the smell permeating the plane was a little overpowering. They were nonetheless grateful to be free, and thanked us for giving them a lift home.

1945. 1st Lt. Joe C. Martin, Jr. 100th Bomb Group, England. Photo courtesy of Matt Mabe.

We were instructed to fly them to Chartres, a Paris suburb. As we made our approach to land on a B-26 field, we skimmed by the tall Gothic spires of the Chartres Cathedral and had to land on landing mats, which had been laid out as a runway. It felt like those mats were rolling up behind us until we came to our hardstand. As our passengers deplaned, most of them kissed the ground and went off singing "La Marseillaise." One fellow even pulled out a homemade French flag. Their happiness was contagious, and I couldn't stop smiling. We'd brought them safely home.

As we lined up behind other B-17s in preparation for our take-off, we watched as several B-26 twin-engine fighter-bombers practiced touch-and-go landings. As we inched forward for take-off, Hank and I decided to show those B-26 pilots what a B-17 could do. We were in one of the old planes with lever-operated turbochargers, and, sometimes, they didn't lock. We forgot to lock the tail wheel, and, with engines roaring and superchargers wide open, we started down the runway. One of the turbocharger levers turned loose, and we began to swerve from one side of the runway to the other. By the time I got the plane under control, we were off the runway and headed toward some parked planes. So, I gave it all we had and took off over them. I'm sure those pilots were as impressed as we were. We'd just dodged a bullet, and I promised myself I'd never do that again.

Chapter 14

Expect a rain of ruin from the air, the like of which has never been seen on this earth.
~ President Harry S. Truman

Final Stages of World War II (May-August 1945)

100th Bomb Group On Parade

On May 26, 1945, the 100th Bomb Group took time out to march. A few of the men, myself included, were awarded the Distinguished Flying Cross. It was an honor to serve my country in time of war; however, I hadn't

expected to receive special recognition for a job I had been trained to do.

It is no coincidence that the four propeller blades on the DFC are in the sign of a cross. When I look up from my desk in my home office to the framed medals on the wall, it always reminds me that on April 7, 1945, God's hand truly was on my shoulder.

The Distinguished Flying Cross, created by Congress more than 90 years ago, is America's oldest military aviation award. The DFC is the fourth highest award for heroism and the highest award for extraordinary aerial achievement.

The cross symbolizes sacrifice, and the propeller symbolizes flight. The combination of those symbols makes clear that the DFC is an award for heroism or achievement for individuals involved in aviation. The ribbon reflects the national colors.

In World War I, aircraft proved their value for reconnaissance and as weapons platforms. Pilots of those primitive flying machines showed both courage and endurance in carrying out air missions. To recognize their gallantry, the Distinguished Flying Cross was created.

~ https://www.dfcsociety.org/pages/the-distinguished-flying-cross-medal

"April 7, 1945: That Me-109 diving into the formation spurting flames all over presented such a vivid picture I'll never forget it. When he hit the ship in front of us [Lt. Joe Martin], his wing (the Me-109) flew off and went over my wing and knocked one of the horizontal stabilizers off the ship behind us in the 'diamond' (Lt. Joe King). Both ships managed to make it back to England and both pilots were awarded the D.F.C. for bringing them back."

~ https://100thbg.com/ Bowman Diary – Page 10 (100th Bomb Group History)

1st Lt. Joe Martin Crew – 26 Combat Missions

2/19/1945: Munster
2/20/1945: Nurnburg
2/21/1945: Nurnburg
2/25/1945: Munich
2/26/1945: Berlin
3/02/1945: Dresden
3/03/1945: Brunswick
3/04/1945: Ulm
3/08/1945: Langendreer
3/09/1945: Frankfurt
3/10/1945: Dortmund
3/14/1945: Seelze
3/15/1945: Oranienburg
3/18/1945: Berlin
3/19/1945: Fulda
3/21/1945: Plauen
3/24/1945: Steenwijk Air Field, Holland
3/24/1945: Ziegenhain Air Field, Holland
3/28/1945: Hanover
3/30/1945: Hamburg
3/31/1945: Zeitz
4/03/1945: Kiel
4/04/1945: Kiel
4/06/1945: Leipzig
4/07/1945: Buchen (Rammed at 15,000 feet)
4/20/1945: Oranienburg (Flew repaired "E-Z Goin'")

~ https://100thbg.com/ (Database)

The 100th on parade 26 May 1945. Courtesy of Jeff Tong

349th Bomb Squadron, my bomb squadron. ~ https://100thbg.com/ (Photo Gallery)

The 100th on parade 26 May 1945, for Brig. Gen. Partridge & Medal Ceremony. ~ https://100thbg.com/ (Photo Gallery)

Casablanca

We continued to ferry soldiers and repatriated civilians to wherever we were instructed to fly them. Then, on June 4, 1945, we flew the last flight of the 95th Bomb Group (35 men) to Casablanca, Africa. We weren't allowed to fly over Spain, so we detoured over France and across the French Riviera, taking a good look at the Mediterranean coast of southeastern France. Then we crossed the Mediterranean Sea to Oran, Algeria. We turned to go across the Sahara Desert and along the Atlas Mountains on the northwestern edge of Africa, spanning Morocco, Algeria, and Tunisia. The low altitude flying at 8,000 feet was so hot you couldn't touch the sides of the uninsulated bomber. So, we had to go up close to 10,000 feet just to stay cool. We couldn't go any higher without oxygen, and we didn't carry enough for all those men. As the crow flies, the trip would normally take nine hours, but this detour took sixteen hours.

The 95th Bomb Group was going by ship from Casablanca across the Atlantic Ocean and home to America. Home. I told myself that it wouldn't be long now before I'd be going home, too. I just didn't know when.

In the meantime, I thought we'd get to see some of Casablanca, but they wouldn't let us cut our engines while the men of the 95th deplaned. We were ordered to take off and fly an hour north to the U.S. Navy base at Rabat, the capital city of Morocco, where we refueled and spent the night. We were each issued one of their white wool blankets to cover up with, but I still nearly froze to death. The Navy made sure we turned those blankets in before we departed. On the flight back to our base, we were given permission to fly over Spain with a direct route to England and Thorpe Abbotts.

As we headed back to the base, it was June 6, 1945, the first anniversary of D-Day. We were nearing the northwestern coast of France, along the Cotentin Peninsula, and we decided to go down for a closer look at the remnant tank traps and a long semi-circle of Navy ships intentionally sunk to form an artificial harbor for some of the landings.

Off in the distance, the top of the Eiffel Tower was barely visible. There was a rumor that an American had flown his P-47 Thunderbolt through the Arc de Triomphe. We wondered if a B-17 would fit through the arch. We made a low-level flight up the Champs-Elysees, which led us to the monument. A huge French tri-color hung in the gateway and, effectively, discouraged us from trying to fly through the arch. As we continued our low-level tour of the city, a P-38 Lightning appeared off our wing, and the fighter pilot gave us a thumbs-up motion, indicating that we should gain altitude. We

headed home to a reception committee waiting at our hardstand. It was decidedly unpleasant.

The War Ends

By the end of July 1945, the Imperial Japanese Navy (IJN) was incapable of conducting major operations, and an Allied invasion of Japan was imminent. Together with the British Empire and China, the United States called for the unconditional surrender of the Japanese armed forces in the Potsdam Declaration on July 26, 1945—the alternative being "prompt and utter destruction." While publicly stating their intent to fight on to the bitter end, Japan's leaders (the Supreme Council for the Direction of the War, also known as the "Big Six") were privately making entreaties to the still-neutral Soviet Union to mediate peace on terms more favorable to the Japanese. Meanwhile, the Soviets were preparing to attack Japanese forces in Manchuria and Korea (in addition to South Sakhalin and the Kuril Islands) in fulfillment of promises they had secretly made to the United States and the United Kingdom at the Tehran and Yalta Conferences. After Japanese leaders flatly rejected the Potsdam Declaration, President Harry S. Truman warned them to "expect a rain of ruin from the air, the like of which has never been seen on this earth." He authorized use of the atomic bomb any time after August 3, 1945.

On August 6, 1945, during the final stages of World War II, the *Enola Gay*—a Boeing B-29 Superfortress bomber piloted by Colonel Paul

Tibbets—became the first aircraft to drop an atomic bomb. The bomb, known as "Little Boy," was targeted at the city of Hiroshima, Japan, and caused unprecedented destruction.

Enola Gay after Hiroshima mission, entering hardstand.
~ https://en.wikipedia.org/wiki/Enola_Gay

Sixteen hours later, President Truman called again for Japan's surrender. Japan refused. A second atomic bomb, known as "Fat Man," was planned for the primary target, Kokura.

However, clouds and drifting smoke resulted in a secondary target, Nagasaki, being bombed from the B-29 *Bockscar* piloted by Major Charles Sweeney on August 9, 1945.

Bockscar after Nagasaki mission, entering hardstand.
~ https://www.atomicheritage.org/history/

Victory over Japan Day or **V-J Day** has been applied to both of the days on which the initial announcement of Japan's surrender was made—to the afternoon of August 15, 1945, in Japan, and, because of time zone differences, to August 14, 1945 (when it was announced in the United States and the rest of the Americas and Eastern Pacific Islands)—as well as to September 2, 1945, when the signing of the surrender document occurred, officially ending World War II.

The Japanese representatives aboard the USS *Missouri* at the Surrender of Japan on September 2, 1945, in Tokyo Bay, Japan.
~ https://en.wikipedia.org/wiki/Victory_over_Japan_Day

The surrender document can be found at: https://www.archives.gov/milestone-documents/surrender-of-japan

Chapter 15

There's no place like home. ~ Dorothy Gale from *The Wizard of Oz*

Building Our Future (1945-1951)

Homeward Bound

In July 1945, since the war in Europe was over, the Army starting sending men home, including my crew. The 100th Bomb Group was assigned to be part of the occupation forces of Germany, and I was to go with them.

As each one of my crew departed, when it came time to say good-bye, what do you say to the men you'd commanded for the last 13 months? The men you'd watched out for and depended on to do their jobs. Men you'd tried hard not to become friends with. I shook their hands and wished them well.

A week later, I was told that they'd refigured my points, and I could go home, too. Like all the other men before me, I packed my gear, took one last look around my quarters, then I hopped in the back of an Army truck that was headed to the train station in London.

A wartime photograph of a US Army Air Force (USAAF) C-46 Commando.
~ https://en.wikipedia.org/wiki/Curtiss_C-46_Commando

My new assignment was an Army personnel depot (disembarkation group) near Blackpool, England (on the Irish Sea coast). There were thousands of men being sent home by different transportation—some by transport planes and some by ship. I spent three weeks at the depot until I received permission to board a C-46 twin-engine transport with about 30 other service men. We flew the northern route toward the good ol' U.S.A.

Our first stop was Greenland. We were stuck there for a few days due to bad weather. They entertained us by taking us ice fishing. The ice was several feet thick everywhere, but we caught some nice flounders.

The next stop was Alaska. We had to fly about fifty miles through a deep canyon to get to the air base. There was only one runway, and it ended in the sea on one end and a huge ice bank on the other, and there was no room for turning around. The pilots who flew that route obviously knew what they were doing, but I had a prayer on my lips and a tight grip on my knees the whole time.

During WWII, photographs of German POWs interned in Canadian camps were taken and reproduced on postcard size stock. The cards provided family and friends with visual assurance of the prisoners' well-being.

~ http://postalhistorycorner.blogspot.ca/2012/07/wwii-real-photo-postcards-german-pows.html

There were a number of Eskimos on the base. We were told that they hung around waiting for their allotment so they could buy whiskey.

I purchased an Eskimo doll from them for Evelyn, which I kept until 2010, when I finally disposed of it because it had greatly deteriorated over time.

Our next stop was an air base in Goose Bay, Labrador, located in the northern part of Canada, to refuel. During the refueling stop, we deplaned and went to the mess hall for a bite to eat. Everywhere you looked, there were men with a P on their backs. They were doing the cooking and maintaining yards with no supervision. I found out that they were German prisoners of war. While they seemed to be as happy as larks, I didn't trust them and stayed away from them.

We re-boarded for the final leg of our trip to the United States. Our final stop was Randolph Air Force Base in San Antonio, Texas. I was allowed to go home to Houston for two months to see my wife and new son, Joe Carl Martin III. Then I returned to Randolph, where I was offered incentives to stay in the service, but I turned them down and was issued an honorable discharge in January 1946. I went home for the final time.

Home Sweet Home

While I was overseas, Evelyn and our son lived with her parents. When I returned home, we continued to live with her parents for about a year. During that time, I decided to go back to the University of Houston on the new GI Bill and finish getting my engineering degree. I also found a part-time job at a sash-and-door mill near the university.

Then Dad asked me to come work with him in the oilfield workover business he'd started. I changed my major from engineering to business, figuring a business degree would be more practical than an engineering degree, so I could help Dad with his new business.

> *Before the war, college and homeownership were, for the most part, unreachable dreams for the average American. Thanks to the GI Bill, millions who would have flooded the job market instead opted for education. In the peak year of 1947, Veterans accounted for 49 percent of college admissions. By the time the original GI Bill ended on July 25, 1956, 7.8 million of 16 million World War II Veterans had participated in an education or training program.*
>
> *Millions also took advantage of the GI Bill's home loan guaranty. From 1944 to 1952, VA backed nearly 2.4 million home loans for World War II Veterans.*
>
> *While Veterans embraced the education and home loan benefits, few collected on one of the bill's most controversial provisions—the unemployment pay. Less than 20 percent of funds set aside for this was used.*
>
> *~ http://www.benefits.va.gov/gibill/history.asp*

My in-laws, Mary and Robert Crotwell, Sr., were very generous in helping Evelyn and me get started. They gave us a plot of land adjoining their property so we could build a house of our own.

I knew nothing about building a house, but a retired builder who lived on the other side of my in-laws showed me everything I needed to know.

Evelyn and I saved our money and bought the wood and supplies we needed until we had enough to completely build a 24-by-24-foot house—about 600 square feet on concrete blocks with crawl space underneath. Very small by today's standards, but it had a living room, an eat-in kitchen (no dining room), a small bedroom, and an even smaller bathroom with a tub/shower. Evelyn worked alongside me whenever she could, and we finished the house in about four months.

Since I didn't want us to have to heat water in the yard, I installed a gas water heater. We used natural gas space heaters during cold spells and window A/C units to cool the house during the summer months.

We built everything except the roof shingles. I hired someone to put cedar shingles on our house. I did the plumbing, electrical, and sewage, which I ran to the middle of the street and tied it into the main sewer line. I did it all with a hand shovel.

Houses on Walthall Drive (Google Image Capture: Dec 2007) ~ https://www.google.com/maps/@29.8322589,-95.3960792,3a,75y,359h,90t/data=!3m6!1e1!3m4!1sVFwE9SIzfRjSu2JKtM_g-w!2e0!7i3328!8i1664!6m1!1e1

Once the house was finished and we'd moved in, I built a one-car garage on the side of the house and made an overhead wooden door that swung up and into the top of the garage. The door was well balanced and easy to open by hand. I poured a concrete driveway in small batches as I had time.

The picture on the previous page was taken in December 2007. The house on the left was my in-laws, which they sold about the same time we sold ours in 1960. At which time, they moved to a nice brick house in a neighborhood off Airline Drive.

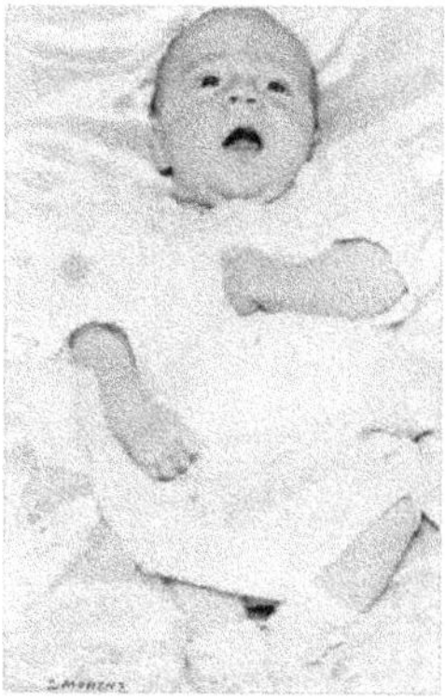
Jerry Wayne Martin

My in-laws have since gone to be with the Lord, and their old, boarded-up house was removed from the property sometime after this photo was taken. Now it is a vacant lot next to the house I had built on the right. You can't see much of the old house because of the trees, and there is a family living there, who have added a ramp.

When our little family of three became four with the birth of our second son, Jerry Wayne Martin, born four days after Christmas 1946, I eventually added a second bedroom on the back of the house for our two boys to share. The room was about 12 by 15 feet.

L-R: Joe Carl III, Evelyn, Jerry

Air Force Reserve

Just months after the surrender of Japan, the USAAF believed that the aggregate wartime experience of army pilots should not be allowed to diminish during peacetime. War Department officials wanted to maintain a pool of combat-tested pilots in the event of a national emergency. Through a Reserve system, pilots would be able to preserve their flying skills with training once a month. The USAAF decided to utilize airfields near large metropolitan areas to maximum population potential.

Where I lived, Reservists from surrounding areas would meet at Ellington Field (about 20 miles southeast of downtown Houston) on selected weekends to fulfill their military commitments. To help funnel Reservists into Houston, the military used a C-47 transport aircraft to shuttle Reservists from as far away as Beaumont and College Station, Texas.

All I had to do was drive to Ellington Field once a month on an assigned weekend to maintain my pilot's license by flying an AT-6 above the Houston skyline, but not over the downtown area. That was restricted air space. I did this until 1951 with the thought that I could be a commercial airline pilot. But, then, my 20-20 vision had started to change and was no longer as sharp as was required for a pilot. Back then, you couldn't wear glasses in the cockpit, and hard plastic contact lenses introduced in the 1950s came too late for me. Plus, my changing vision kept me out of the Korean War (1950-1953), which really relieved Evelyn and my parents. And, I have to admit that I wasn't looking forward to going back to war again.

USAAF AT-6Cs near Luke Field (Arizona), 1943 ~ https://en.wikipedia.org/wiki/North_American_T-6_Texan

Ellington Field in Houston, Texas, has a unique history that mirrors the course of 20th century American military history. For 81 years, Ellington Field served the United States Army and Air Force through times of war, cold war, and peace. Over the past 8 decades, the airfield has functioned in a variety of operational roles: as an active-duty base, an Air Force Reserve base, and an Air National Guard base. Overall, Ellington Field's economic, political, and technological impact on the development of south Texas cannot be underestimated. While most military facilities built in 1917 to train pilots for combat in the First World War have long since disappeared, Ellington Field remains active as a private field that serves the military, commercial, and general aviation needs of Houston.

~ https://historycollection.jsc.nasa.gov/JSCHistoryPortal/history/ellington/ Ellington.pdf (60-page document published in 1999)

The North American Aviation T-6 Texan is a single-engine advanced trainer aircraft used to train pilots of the United States Army Air Forces (USAAF), United States Navy, Royal Air Force, and other air forces of the British Commonwealth during World War II and into the 1970s. Designed by North American Aviation, the T-6 is known by a variety of designations depending on the model and operating air force. The United States Army Air Corps (USAAC) and USAAF designated it as the AT-6, the United States Navy the SNJ, and British Commonwealth air forces, the Harvard, the name by which it is best known outside of the US. After 1962, US forces designated it the T-6. It remains a popular warbird aircraft used for airshow demonstrations and static displays. It has also been used many times to simulate various Japanese aircraft, including the Mitsubishi A6M Zero in movies depicting World War II in the Pacific.

~ https://en.wikipedia.org/wiki/North_American_T-6_Texan

Though contact lenses seem to be a recent phenomenon, the famous Italian architect, mathematician, and inventor Leonardo da Vinci (1452-1519) produced the first known sketches (in 1508) that suggested the optics of the human eye could be altered by placing the cornea directly in contact with water....

In 1827, English astronomer Sir John Herschel proposed the idea of making a mold of a person's eyes. Such molds would enable the production of corrective lenses that could conform to the front surface of the eye. But it was more than 50 years later that someone actually produced such lenses, and there is some controversy about who did it first....

In 1948, California optician Kevin Tuohy (1919-1968) introduced the first contact lenses that resembled modern gas permeable (GP) contact lenses of today. These all-plastic lenses were called "corneal" contact lenses because they were smaller in diameter than previous contact lenses and covered only the clear front surface of the eye (the cornea)....

Properly fitted, corneal PMMA contact lenses could be worn for 16 hours or longer. Advances in lens manufacturing techniques and fitting expertise among eye doctors led to the mass appeal of these hard plastic contact lenses in the 1950s and 1960s.

~ https://www.allaboutvision.com/contacts/faq/when-invented.htm

Chapter 16

My father taught me to work; he did not teach me to love it.
~ Abraham Lincoln

Back to the Oil Fields (1946-1986)

Faith, Hope, and Love

During 1946, we started attending Airline Drive Baptist Church. The church was started by 21 families on February 8, 1942, and Pastor Lee Roy Pearson served until March 1943, when he resigned to go into the Marine Corps during World War II. I used to run into Rev. Pearson every now and then, before he retired to East Texas. He passed away in March 2017 at the age of 98.

After Rev. Pearson joined the Marines, Rev. Culbert came to be the pastor. He was a real fire-and-brimstone preacher. He served in that capacity until about 1953, at which time he was asked to resign due to some unchristian-like practices.

Rev. W.A. Curtis was hired to replace Rev. Culbert shortly after he resigned. I was made a deacon that same year, and we baptized 167 souls. In 1955, we added a two-story Sunday school building at the rear of the church, and, in 1960, I was elected church treasurer.

The demographics of the neighborhood where the church was located had started changing during the late 1960s, from predominately white to black, and, in 1971, we sold the church to a black family by the name of Hunter. The church was renamed the Hunter Memorial Church of God in Christ.

Our church relocated to the bankrupt Cole Creek Baptist Church on Tidwell in May 1968. We paid off the $100,000 note and changed the name to First Baptist Church Northwest. I continued to serve as treasurer for our new church.

Hunter Memorial Church of God in Christ (Google Image Capture: 12/2007)
~ https://www.google.com/maps/place/4127+Airline+Dr,+Houston,+TX+77022/

In 1975, we built a gymnasium (100' x 60' x 20' high) at the rear of the church for $60,000 for the youth, in anticipation of a large influx, but it never happened. Rev. Curtis had been teaching part-time at Prairie View A&M to supplement his salary from the church. In 1977, he decided to resign as our pastor and teach full-time at the college.

I was now a member of the Pulpit Committee, and, as soon as Rev. Curtis gave us notice that he was leaving, we started looking for a new pastor. We went to hear a young preacher, just out of the Marine Corps, having served in the Vietnam War, by the name of Johnny Paul Price. He wasn't an ordained minister, but all five of us on the Pulpit Committee agreed that he was the one we needed, because when he preached, he spoke from the heart.

We invited him to speak before our congregation, and, in 1978, the members voted to elect Bro. Price as our new pastor. He was eventually ordained, and, later, the church elected to send him to college to get a theology doctorate. His title changed from Rev. Price to Dr. Price, and, when he returned to full-time preaching, he came with a new philosophy about the direction of our church. He felt we should resign our fellowship from the Southern Baptist Convention and embrace The Foursquare Church.

Of course, we'd never heard of this organization and weren't sure we wanted to go in that direction, so Dr. Price resigned as our pastor. However, the church didn't want him to leave. The membership voted for him to stay, one hundred percent.

This was a huge change for our church. After we broke away from the Southern Baptist Convention, it became necessary for Dr. Price, Bro. Cleve Ferrel, and myself to assume ownership of the property for the next two years while we learned about and transitioned to The Foursquare Church during the early 1980s.

Houston Northwest Foursquare/Life Family Church (Google Image Capture: 10/2015) ~ https://www.google.com/maps/place/6870+W+Tidwell+Rd, +Houston+TX+77092/

We learned that there is a four-stage development model that identifies four phases of progressive maturity in the Christian Life—becoming disciples and learning to evangelize, becoming leaders who serve family and church, helping to establish other churches, and reaching out to other cultures and languages. It was not unlike the Baptist Church philosophy, so we joined The Foursquare Church, turned over the ownership of the property to them, and changed the name of our church to Houston Northwest Foursquare Church also known as Life 4SQ Church, or just Life Church. I remained the treasurer until 1998. Dr. Price served as our pastor for 35 years and retired in 2013.

Carl Martin Oil Well Service

When Dad quit Sinclair Oil and Gas Company and went into business for himself in 1946, he had my sister Tomalene—a freshman at the University of Houston and his partner in his new company—find some land on which they could set up their office. She found a house and some adjoining property on Luke Street.

Sinclair had stopped doing their own repair work on their oil and gas wells and struck a deal with Dad. They agreed to give most of their equipment to Dad if he would contract to do the work for them, because that's what he was doing before he quit. All he had to do was buy a pulling unit and derrick and went to work.

A pulling unit, also known as a workover rig, is one of the mechanical oilfield applications used to remove the casing and other tubing apparatuses inside a wellbore.

A pulling unit is called in when a wellbore shows signs of internal damage, such as an obvious leak or a sudden drop in pressure of the drilling fluid at the surface. When a wellbore is displaying production problems that can't be repaired through more simple means, the unit is charged with physically lifting the casing and any of the drilling equipment that appears to be damaged out of the wellbore to be examined and repaired in a timely manner.

In 1949, after getting my business degree, I went into the oilfield workover business as a partner with my father and my sister. Tomalene's husband W.S. "Buster" Kennedy joined the business in 1952.

After I went to work with Dad, we bought another pulling unit, derrick, pump, and tools. We purchased a small, one-story office building on North Shepherd and leased some space across the street to work on the rigs.

All the signage and rigs were painted "Carl Martin Yellow," a special blend of yellow paint. It was recognized by all the major oil companies we did business with throughout Texas and Louisiana.

I started at the bottom. I went to work on one of the rigs, working on the floor with the rough necks in order to learn everything there was to know. I went home every night with oil-soaked clothes.

After learning how to run a rig, I started looking after all the rigs and calling on other oil companies for business. We had acquired about twelve working rigs and other equipment, and then we began drilling oil wells, too. I was hardly ever home. Our business had spread so far, sometimes I flew to a town near the rig and rented a car to check on the rig and visit with the customer. We had one rig that stayed right near the Mexico border for about a year, and the company man would kid me about taking the rig to Mexico if I didn't visit him more often.

We lost one of our rigs to a butane fire when oil leaked from an underground storage well. As the sun came up, the natural gas rose up into the power lines, sparked, and exploded. The heat melted all the aluminum parts, and the metal ran off like water. Insurance on the well took care of replacing the rig. If fire broke out while we were on a well site, we put out the fire ourselves. No time to call Red Adair. We could lose the well.

In 1960, we bought 20 acres of land along I-45 North near Gulf Bank Road and built a big shop to assemble and service the rigs out of the weather and a place to build our own tanks, pumps, and substructures.

That was also the same year that Mother passed away on May 21, 1960. Cleo Mallory Martin was 56 years old.

In 1963, while servicing one of the rigs, we stopped for lunch and someone turned on the radio for some C&W music. Instead, the news was reporting that President John F. Kennedy had been assassinated in Dallas. It was a somber Thanksgiving that year.

Not long after that, the Vietnam War, a conflict in Vietnam, Laos, and Cambodia from November 1, 1955 to the fall of Saigon on April 30, 1975, heated up under President Lyndon B. Johnson. It was the second of the Indochina Wars and was officially fought between North Vietnam and South Vietnam with the support of American troops.

Many Americans opposed our involvement in the war. There were daily protests, except for one day in July of 1969, when the world stood still and stared at their TV sets as astronaut Neil Armstrong became the first human being to walk on the moon, marking the historic moment with the phrase: "That's one small step for man, one giant leap for mankind."

During this time, Dad decided to take a backseat and turned over control of our workover business to me and appointed me President.

On September 28, 1979, Dad went out in his boat on the Trinity River to do some fishing and check his trout lines. When one of his fishing buddies went out to check on him, the friend found Dad in his captain's chair, gloved hands clutching the steering wheel. He'd had a heart attack. We buried him next to Mother in the family plot at Brookside Cemetery. Joe Carl Martin, Sr., was 80 years old.

Since the early 1900s, when Dad struck out on his own to work on that pipeline, the price of oil and the number of wells drilled has fluctuated. However, by 1970, onshore oil production had dropped to 13,063,182,000 barrels due to increasing regulations and cheaper oil being imported from the Organization of Petroleum Exporting Countries (OPEC). Then in the 1980s, oil prices began to drastically decline, prompting OPEC to cut production in order to bolster the value of its lifeblood. In late 1985, Saudi Arabia abandoned its strategy of propping up prices and, instead, began increasing production in order to increase market share. By July 1986, the average per barrel free on board (FOB) price for OPEC crude oil had dropped from $23.29 to $9.85 in December 1985, a 58% decline in a matter of months. Initially, nearly 2,300 rigs were drilling wells in the U.S.; a year later, there were less than 1,000.

Unemployment in the oil and gas industry shot up, with an article from the *L.A. Times* published in June 1986, saying the oil and gas industry had laid off 100,000 workers in the first five months of the year.

During this time, all work on domestic oil wells came to a halt, effectively, putting us out of business. We couldn't keep our employees busy. Fortunately, we were the only workover company that had a retirement plan for our employees, so we closed down Carl Martin Oil Well Service, auctioned off all of our equipment, and retired.

Since everything was paid for, we kept the 20 acres and the big shop until some years later, when we leased the land and shop to a truck company, which later bought it from us. The profits were split between me and Tomalene, as per Dad's will. A few years later, the truck company sold out to AutoNation who redeveloped the property.

Carl Martin Oil Well Service only had two fatalities during the entire time we were in business. One was a derrick man who had taken too many no-dose tablets on a weekend trip and was not in shape to go up in the derrick on Monday, but no one knew that until it was too late. The other death was my uncle Orville Mallory. While driving a workover rig through a mud hole, the rig started to tip over and he jumped out of the protective cab. The rig crushed him in the mud. We laid him to rest in the family plot, where his wife Ida joined him a few years later.

Two Additions to Our Family

My family in June 1959:
L-R Joe Carl III, Darline, Evelyn, Linda, Jerry

In 1956, we were awarded two baby girls from a family court in Bryan, Texas—Linda, 18 months, and Darline, 3 years old. The girls' mother was a distant cousin of Evelyn's mother, which is how they came to live with us. We were not allowed to adopt the girls. The court took them back once and tried to reunite the family, but it didn't work out, so the court asked us to take them back, and they remained with us as a part of our family. They called us Mother and Daddy.

A New Home

In 1960, I built us a new and larger home on Hollyvale Drive on an acre of land. I used a contractor and his crew, but I oversaw the construction.

The house wasn't complete yet when it started snowing the morning of February 12, 1960, and continued throughout the night. The storm rolled through southeast Texas and dropped 11 inches of snow in Livingston and 6 inches of snow in Cleveland. The 4.4 inches that blanketed Houston was the highest amount of snow since the record-setting storm of 1895, which dumped a whopping 20 inches of snow in Houston on Valentine's Day.

Once it stopped snowing, we drove over to check on our house.

Unlike our first house, this new house had 1,997 square feet and was all brick with central air and heat. It had an attached two-car garage, a formal living room, large den and open kitchen combination, separate laundry room off the kitchen, three bedrooms, and two full bathrooms. It was everything I'd always wanted to give Evelyn. And she had a ball decorating her new home.

Because there were no trees, I planted a few—pecan, peach, fig, lemon, and a grapefruit tree. I, also, planted plum and crabapple trees, which produced fruit for two years, then they died.

Hurricane Carla ~ September 1961

The local news stations had a lot of people concerned about Hurricane Carla, myself included. I'd faced a lot of things in my life, but this was my first hurricane, and I took the warnings seriously.

My brother-in-law's family owned some land with a house on it in Corrigan, about 95 miles northeast of Houston. Buster drove Tomalene, their two daughters, our two sons, and our two foster daughters to Corrigan to stay for about a week. Evelyn and I stayed behind to protect our home. Dad and I shut down the workover rigs and sent the crews home, then we monitored the storm.

Fortunately, we suffered minimal damage, compared to others. Once the hurricane had passed, our family came home, and we went back to work, making repairs as needed.

Hurricane Carla hit the Texas coast as a Category 4 hurricane on September 10, 1961, causing the deaths of 46 people, 465 injured, and an estimated $300 million dollars in total damage. Except for the Great Galveston Storm of 1900, it was the worst hurricane ever to hit Texas at that time.

Hurricane watches were issued for the entire Texas coast on the 8th of September and warnings were issued on the 9th, which prompted the evacuation of half a million people, the largest evacuation in United States history up to that time.

Carla was an extremely large hurricane with devastating effects from the winds and storm surge. The highest sustained wind speeds reported were 115 mph at Matagorda, 110 mph at Victoria, and 88 mph at Galveston. Extreme peak wind gusts were estimated to be near 170 mph at Port Lavaca as the wind equipment blew away after reading 153 mph.

Carla's storm surge devastated the Texas coast, rising to 10 feet above normal along a 300-mile swath from Port Aransas to Sabine Pass. The hurricane spawned 18 tornadoes with 10 in Louisiana and 8 in Texas.

~ https://www.weather.gov/crp/hurricanecarla

Chapter 17

Go into all the world and preach the gospel to all creation.
~ Mark 16:15

Mission Trips (1980-1992)

Mount St. Helens Blows Her Top

I've owned a couple of different boats in my lifetime. One was a 16-foot kit boat with two outboard motors. Someone stole the motors one night while it was parked in the driveway of our Hollyvale home. That's when I built a boat garage off the left side of the property and separate from the house.

Another boat I owned was a 21-foot fiberglass boat with a canvas top and an indoor toilet. It was powered with two 50 HP outboard engines, and our boys learned to water ski. We were members of a boat club and toured the Gulf Coast from Brownsville, Texas, to New Orleans, Louisiana.

But, mostly, I enjoyed fishing in the bays around Galveston. Sometimes, our boys went with me. Sometimes, it was just me and the quiet of the early morning dawn as I watched the sun come up and thanked the Lord for all His blessings.

We also owned a 35-foot motorhome and used it on family trips. We traveled all over the western part of the United States, including Disneyland in California and the Grand Canyon. We went to Florida to visit Walt Disney World when it first opened. The motorhome also came in handy when Evelyn and I went deer hunting. On one hunting trip, Evelyn shot two deer with her Single Action 243 Winchester.

We used the motorhome to do some evangelistic work with Bro. A.B. Lightfoot in Oregon and Washington State. Evelyn and I in our motorhome and Bro. Lightfoot with his wife Rose in their motorhome, along with a few other families, were there the week Mount St. Helens erupted.

At about 8:30 am on Sunday, May 18, 1980, a 5.1 magnitude earthquake caused the entire north face of the Mount St. Helens volcano to slip away in the largest observed landslide in recorded history.

Plinian eruption column from May 18, 1980, Mount St. Helens. Aerial view from the Southwest.
~ https://volcanoes.usgs.gov/volcanoes/st_helens/st_helens_geo_hist_99.html

A wave of hot gases, molten snow, and steam, combined with soil and rock, ripped across the land at more than 300 mph. When it was over, the mountain was about 1,300 feet shorter.

The countryside was turned into a wasteland. Hundreds of homes were destroyed, along with scores of bridges, and about 200 miles of roads.

In all, the volcano caused over a billion dollars in damage, yet most tragic of all were the 57 deaths caused by the event.

We'd arrived a couple of days after the initial explosion. There was so much ash piled up, it looked like a foot or two of dirty snow had fallen from a recent snowstorm. We were not able to enter the area until the roads were cleared. We prayed for everyone affected by the eruption of the volcano. Then we rolled up our sleeves to help wherever we could. And, along the way, we won a few souls for the Lord.

Building Churches in Mexico

I was made the Missions Director of Life 4SQ Church, and we felt led to build churches in Mexico. Our first venture was sponsored by Lakewood Church, pastored by Rev. John Osteen (Pastor Joel Osteen's father and before they turned the Compaq Center—formerly The Summit—into a church). John Osteen's Missions Director advised me on what we needed to do. He helped us get started and funded the first church we built in 1985.

Evelyn and I and a group of about 20 men and some of the wives set out in a convoy of trucks, minivans, and trailers carrying all the supplies and tools we would need to build a 12-by-30-foot church, using the building plans provided to us by Lakewood's Missions Director. I'd learned a lot about building a simple structure when I built my first home, plus some of the other guys had carpentry or construction experience, so we felt sure we could build a church.

Inside Mexico, we traveled along Highway 1 to a small place about 100 miles from Ciudad Victoria and located in the mountains. We made our way up a narrow, crooked road to about 9,000 feet. Then about 20 miles more on a primitive dirt road to the village of Mama Leon located in the desert.

Through one of our men who spoke Spanish, the people told us that it had not rained in four years. Would you believe, it started raining the first day we arrived. It rained all day and all night. We had no tents, so we slept in our vehicles.

The people begged us not to pray for the rain to stop. However, once the rain did stop, we had to wait until the ground was completely dry because we couldn't walk around. The surface was some sort of clay—sticky and slippery—and the people made bricks out of it.

After we finished building the church, the local pastor held their first service to a packed crowd with other people looking through the windows. There was a group of young men called the White Shirts who'd hung around watching us build the church, but they wouldn't come inside, and they never gave us any problems.

Me standing to the side of the first church we built in 1985.

About a year later, one of the men who'd helped build the first church, Hollis Brewer, returned with me and

Plaque inside the church: "This temple is presented by Christian Life Ministries by the Holy Spirit."

Evelyn, along with a Mexican preacher from Lakewood Church, to dedicate this new church. The preacher held a service, and all but three people accepted Christ as their Savior.

While we were there, we met a missionary and his wife, Gerald and Clara Brown, who lived in Ciudad Victoria. The Browns provided the gospel and food, and had already built twenty churches in Mexico. We asked them for their help with our mission to build more churches, and they were glad to work with us. Gerald told us which villages needed a church. He planned it out, acting as our interpreter and introducing us to the village leaders.

Evelyn traveled with me on every trip, wielding a hammer right alongside the other women who helped nail on the wood siding. The men did the heavy lifting of framing the churches and putting on the tin roof. We also built bench pews and a lectern where the preacher stood before his congregation and conducted the church services.

This church was built in 1987 in the suburbs of Ciudad Victoria, Mexico. Left: Inside the church with me at the front presenting the church to its pastor. Right: We built a fence around the church to keep out the animals.

When we first started making the trips to Mexico, we would drive straight through from Houston to our final destination. But the Mexican Army would stop us in the middle of the night and search our vehicles for illegal drugs or guns. Or bandits would rob us. So, we decided to stop in McAllen, Texas, spend the night, then start out early the next morning to reach our various destinations before nightfall. It wasn't much safer to travel by day because it cost about a hundred dollars a trailer load, which they called a tax, but it was really a bribe.

We built thirty churches over an eight-year period, each church taking about four or five days to build. The first twenty churches we built had shuttered windows. The last ten we added glass windows.

Mr. and Mrs. Brown still keep in touch, and many of the churches we built still exist. The Browns no longer live in Mexico. It became too dangerous for them. They now live in Guatemala and fly back and forth to the U.S. Their missionary work includes their grown children who help them collect as many things as they can to provide for the people who need it.

This is one of the churches we'd built. I'm standing to the far left wearing a white shirt and cowboy hat. Evelyn is on the right side, in front, kneeling in a group of three women. She's the one on the right.

Teddy Roosevelt and His Rough Riders

We once spent a week in Guatemala helping another missionary couple, Mr. & Mrs. Stoffason, rebuild their hospital in the jungle that the rebels had damaged. I built a steel tower and put a 400-gallon water tank on top so they could have flowing water into their house and hospital.

It was about a 1,500-mile trip by truck. I carried the material on a trailer through Mexico and Belize. The last 100 miles was a dirt road that ended at a river. We loaded all the material on some 40-foot long boats with outboard motors and traveled down the river for about 35 miles. The river was wide and deep, and the currents were swift. It was real jungle, because we heard animals during the night.

We were told that this area was the place where Teddy Roosevelt trained his Rough Riders before invading Cuba in 1898 in the Spanish-American War.

The Rough Riders Regiment was the name given to the First U.S. Volunteer Cavalry under the leadership of Lieutenant Colonel Theodore Roosevelt, who had resigned his position as Assistant Secretary of the Navy in May 1898 in order to join the volunteer cavalry. The original plan for this unit called for filling it with men from the Indian Territory, New Mexico, Arizona, and Oklahoma. However, once the adventurous Roosevelt joined the group, it quickly became the place for a mix of troops ranging from Ivy League athletes to glee-club singers to Texas Rangers and Indians. They made headlines for their role in the Battle of San Juan Hill, which became the stuff of legend thanks to Roosevelt's writing ability and reenactments filmed long after. He also had a photographic memory, which gave him the ability to recall text or images with great precision.

Then, on September 14, 1901, with the assassination of President William McKinley, Theodore Roosevelt, as McKinley’s vice president, became the 26th and youngest President (not quite 43) in the Nation’s history (1901-1909).

Chapter 18

I have fought the good fight, I have finished the course,
I have kept the faith. ~ 2 Timothy 4:7

Evelyn
(1992-1994)

Unexpected News

Evelyn and I were married for 51 years and 5 months. During that time, we had weathered many ups and downs, facing everything together. There was only one thing we couldn't overcome. Cancer.

We'd returned from one of our trips, and she'd developed a dry cough and said she couldn't catch her breath, so I drove her directly to the hospital. In the emergency room, the doctor ordered a chest x-ray, which showed that Evelyn had fluid around her lungs, causing the difficulty with her breathing. They had to insert a tube into her chest cavity to drain the fluid so she could breathe.

The fluid was sent to pathology where it was tested, and it came back positive for cancer cells.

We were told that the cancer had caused a pleural effusion, which is a buildup of extra fluid in the space between the lungs and the chest wall. This condition is a sign that the cancer has spread to other areas of the body, which meant the doctor had to find the source of where the initial cancer was located.

Evelyn underwent several types of x-rays and blood tests to determine what type of cancer she had.

The diagnosis was ovarian cancer. However, she hadn't had any pain in that area, so we were surprised by the diagnosis. We learned that this is common with ovarian cancer. There are no symptoms until it spreads and involves other parts of the body, like the fluid build-up in her chest.

She underwent a biopsy to confirm the doctor's initial diagnosis. They started her on chemotherapy to keep the fluid from building up again and to keep the cancer from spreading.

The doctor didn't give us any false hope. He gave us the facts and what we could expect from the treatment he had recommended. It was basically a wait-and-see-what-happens course of treatment—chemotherapy and radiation now to help shrink the cancerous tumor and possible surgery later to remove it.

Of course, we prayed for a good outcome, but, ultimately, we put the decision in God's hands.

All this testing happened over a period of several days. Once we had decided on a course of action, we contacted our grown children, who came directly to the hospital to lend their love and support.

Our 50th Wedding Anniversary

After various rounds of chemotherapy and radiation, Evelyn was allowed to come home where I cared for her and prepared her meals that she could tolerate as she dealt with the nauseous after-effects of chemotherapy.

During this time of uncertainty, our church hosted a party in the Fellowship Hall to celebrate our 50th anniversary. Evelyn wore one of her looser dresses since she'd become swollen because of the drugs. Plus, her thick auburn hair had begun to lose its luster and eventually fell out. We bought a nice wig, so she could look her best for the party.

L-R: Me, Evelyn, Buster, and Tomalene at our 50th Wedding Anniversary party.

She barely ate or drank anything, but she smiled a lot and accepted hugs and kisses from everyone there.

Going Home

Evelyn eventually had a complete hysterectomy, and part of her colon where the cancer had spread was removed. She was fitted with a colostomy bag, and I was instructed on how to change it for her when she was allowed to come home at various times.

Over the two years we fought the cancer, Evelyn spent 360 days in the hospital. And I stayed with her to make sure she got the care she deserved. I slept on one of those leather easy chairs that makes into a bed, sleeping when she slept. Of course, you really don't get much sleep in the hospital with the nurses checking Evelyn's vitals every few hours and changing her colostomy bag and replacing the empty IV bags for full ones.

During this time, I fought with the hospital food division because the food they served the patients was terrible. Even I wouldn't eat it. I began bringing food from home that I knew Evelyn would be able to eat.

I checked into what the food problem was and found out that the hospital was serving catered food, not food prepared fresh in the hospital kitchen. One patient across the hall from Evelyn threw his food tray at a nurse, along with a few other things, to make his point about how terrible the food was.

I called the CEO of the hospital and made an official complaint. Changes were made, and they started preparing fresh food in the hospital kitchen.

During the latter months as Evelyn's health continued to decline, when we knew we were just marking time, our daughter-in-law Janice volunteered to stay with Evelyn on the weekends so I could go home and take care of things at the house. Janice was working a full-time job, so this was the only time she could spare.

Janice did her best to make Evelyn comfortable. She'd arrive at the hospital on Friday evenings and sleep on that same leather chair, getting up with Evelyn during the night just like I did. She bought some different colored turbans for Evelyn to wear, since she was completely bald. It was her hope to cheer Evelyn, and I think it did.

When Evelyn was up to it, Janice would give her massages as well as manicures and pedicures. They took occasional, short walks down the hospital corridor with the assistance of one of the nurses, who pushed the mobile IV pole.

On Saturday mornings, knowing that she always had visitors, Evelyn would wear one of the turbans or her wig, which Janice would fluff up and made sure it looked nice. She also helped Evelyn with her make-up. She had no eyebrows, so Janice would use Evelyn's eyebrow pencil to create some for her. Then she'd apply a little blush to her pale cheeks and lipstick to her lips.

And when her visitors arrived, Evelyn was ready to greet them with her best smile, putting her visitors at ease. Janice would slip away for a cup of coffee at the nurses' station or take a walk around the hospital to give Evelyn and her friends or other family members the privacy they needed.

In the evenings, Evelyn liked to read her Bible and pray, not for a cure, but for courage to face what she knew was coming. And she did.

Evelyn accepted her home going with grace and the love of her family surrounding her on July 15, 1994.

Chapter 19

I wait for You, O Lord; You will answer, O Lord my God.
~ Psalm 38:15 (NIV)

Virginia (1995-Present)

Heart Trouble

After Evelyn's death, I found it impossible to live in the house I'd built for her. So, I moved our motorhome over to our church and stayed there most of the time, making repairs where needed and remaining faithful in my worship of the Lord.

In February 1995, my heart became weak, and I would pass out. Since our family doctor had passed away not long after Evelyn, I went to a new doctor. He ran tests and said I had atrial fibrillation and that I needed a pacemaker. He called a heart specialist just down the hall from his office who immediately took me in. That doctor said I shouldn't go home, but that I should go directly to the hospital where he would install a pacemaker.

Fortunately, the medical professional building I was in was right next to the hospital where the pacemaker was installed. I was given a mild sedative and watched on a television monitor as the doctor inserted a wire into my heart. I had to stay overnight to make sure the pacemaker was working properly and doing what it was supposed to, and then I went home. That's when I called my family members to let them know what had happened, and that I was just fine. Over the past 18 years (as of 2013), I've had two pacemakers installed. And I'm still doing just fine.

During the summer of 1995, Darline, our elder foster daughter, who'd married some time back and had three boys, asked if her two oldest sons could live with me at the house. So I moved back home. Having others in the house made it easier to live there.

Then in the latter part of 1995, Bro. Cleve Ferrell asked me to serve on the Board of the Harris County Emergency Corps. While on the Board, I took EMT classes to be able to fill in on an ambulance. Needing something else to do, I began making repairs around the office building. I had to consult with the office manager, who was a pretty lady by the name of Virginia Hetzel, a divorcee with a grown son and daughter, and one son in high school. Virginia was also a trained paramedic.

Sometimes, we would work late, and I would take her to lunch or dinner, then it became a regular thing. We really enjoyed each other's company, and she gave me a reason to smile and enjoy life again.

On December 31, 1996, after leaving a New Year's Eve Party, I asked Virginia to marry me. We were married by Dr. Price on April 26, 1997.

I moved into Virginia's home with her and her youngest son, David, who was about to graduate high school. Then he went off to college at Sam Houston State University.

Virginia's two other grown children, Thomas and Lisa, live in California.

We lived in Virginia's home for about two years and put the house in top shape so she could sell it. Then we moved into a two-bedroom, wood-frame house on Luke Street off North Shepherd. During this time, I sold the house on Hollyvale to my son Joe Carl III and his wife Suzanne.

Carl Martin Oil Well Service owned the house on Luke and the land that adjoined the property where our original office headquarters were located on North Shepherd.

Tomalene and Buster and their two daughters, Wilma and Gale, lived on Sam Street, in the house just behind the house on Luke. Wilma married and had a daughter named Kimberly, who is married now with children of her own.

Our house on Luke Street (Google Image Capture: 3/2011). The house is hidden behind trees and the white picket fence. There's a detached three-car garage on the left where we parked our 25-ft Winnebago motorhome. ~ https://www.google.com/maps

When Gale married, she and her husband Brent moved into the house next door to Tomalene and Buster. Gale and Brent have a daughter, April, and a son, James.

After Virginia and I moved into the house on Luke, we painted it inside and out. Virginia did a nice job of decorating the inside and making it feel like home. I built a porch on the back of the house, and we added a hot tub behind that with a nice gazebo-type cover that I built. I planted a small vegetable garden in the backyard and rose bushes on the garage side of the house where we parked our cars and entered through the side back door.

I planted crepe myrtles on the other side of the driveway and added a white picket fence along the front and down one side of the yard.

In 2002, my sister Tomalene Martin Kennedy passed away, followed by her husband W.S. "Buster" Kennedy in 2007.

In 2009, all three families—Virginia and me, Gale and Brent, and Wilma—decided to move to a gated community in Spring, Texas (just north of Houston). There was a new subdivision being developed, and we picked out our own floorplans and the lots where we wanted to live. We're now within walking distance of all three homes.

We sold our old houses on Sam and Luke streets to a house-moving company, and then we eventually sold the property to a trucking company.

Swing Your Partner

Shortly after Virginia and I were married in 1997, we took up square dancing. We took lessons with the Tomball Promenaders and the Bluebonnet Squares. We tried round dancing, but we never did well at it.

We enjoyed the camaraderie more than anything else, especially when I had to sit down more often than I was able to dance. Arthritis had settled in my knees and made it difficult to move as quickly as I needed to when swinging my partner.

Sometimes, we'd just sit along the wall and watch the others dance. We'd clap to the beat of the music and have a good time. We eventually quit going altogether in 2013 when I had to start using a walker to get around.

Since then, I've taken up reading cowboy books that I check out at our local library. I read about six books every week, and I've since purchased an e-book reader. The old eyes aren't what they used to be, so I can bump up the font size and still enjoy some good stories.

Virginia and I enjoyed our weekly potluck dinner and Bible study led by Bro. Skeet Garret at Life Church, until the church was sold. Occasionally, we attend Cypress Creek Christian Church and enjoy their monthly senior luncheon. We attend various events by way of a chartered bus for seniors. And, in 2013, I was able to renew my driver's license.

9/11

On September 11, 2001, ten days after my 78th birthday, our nation was attacked for the second time during my lifetime. The World Trade Center towers in New York City were brought down by terrorists aboard two commercial airliners, followed by another airliner hitting The Pentagon in Arlington County, Virginia, and another one brought down by the brave passengers aboard United Airlines Flight 93, crashing into a field in Pennsylvania. The attacks killed almost 3,000 people. Our nation is still under threat of attack, not only from outside our nation, but from within.

80 Years Young

In 2003, for my 80th birthday, Virginia had planned a surprise birthday party, but she had to cancel it. I had a gallbladder attack and had to have it removed. Some weeks later, Joe and Jerry and their wives treated Virginia and me to dinner at my favorite place, Red Lobster. After dinner, Suzanne, Joe's wife, presented me with two United States Air Force albums.

Suzanne had assembled one album of my war years, and the other album

L-R: Suzanne; Joe Carl III; Joe Carl, Jr.; Virginia; Jerry; Janice

of my childhood and family memories. Together, both albums told the complete story of my 80 years on this earth. She later assembled a third album of the leftovers that would not fit in the other two. I marveled at her creativeness, and I appreciated it very much. Thank you, Suzanne.

World War II Memorial

On May 29, 2004, Virginia and I, along with my grandson Dante Martin and his father-in-law Owen Tibbetts, attended the dedication of the National World War II Memorial in Washington, D.C.

We were seated with other veterans fairly close to the front where we could see President George W. Bush, the actor Tom Hanks, and other dignitaries as they spoke.

The World War II Memorial truly honors those who made the ultimate sacrifice for our great nation.

Fourth of July Honors

On July 3, 2005, Janice invited Virginia and me to attend their July 4th Sunday service with her and Jerry at Berachah Church. Janice had borrowed the two albums that Suzanne had assembled and had the album with my years in the Army Air Corps on display in the foyer of the church.

Outside on the quadrangle at the edge of the parking lot, there were various military vehicles assembled for church members to view. This was part of a teaching moment for the Prep School children (Sunday school at my church) to understand that freedom is not free.

After the colors were posted by uniformed members of our armed services, the teachers presented their program about what our flag represents and the sacrifices made by our military for the freedom we enjoy.

And then they called my name to recognize my service during World War II. I had no idea that they would honor me for my service.

I had attended Berachah Church a few years back at Janice and Jerry's

That's me in a white dress shirt at the edge of the tent just before my name was called.

invitation to hear their previous pastor, R.B. Thieme, Jr., teach the Word of God. I learned that Pastor Thieme had also served in the Army Air Corps during World War II and was in charge of training air cadets at Luke Field in Arizona. By the end of the war, he had risen to the rank of Lieutenant Colonel, but now Colonel Thieme is with the Lord.

The Panama Canal

Over the years, Virginia and I have taken a number of cruises. One cruise was to Alaska in the summertime, but it was still very cold. Had some spectacular views, though.

The most recent cruise we took was in 2014 to the Panama Canal, but we never made it.

Me & Virginia on Alaskan cruise.

The Panama Canal cruise left out of Los Angeles, and on the third day as we were nearing Huatulco, Mexico, I started having breathing problems. The medical staff onboard the ship put me on oxygen and some kind of medication that gave me some relief, but they really didn't want to deal with my medical issues because of my pacemaker. They wanted me to see a heart doctor at the hospital in Huatulco. This little town has since become one of their ports of call for cruise passengers to visit. At the time we were there, it wasn't.

Virginia explained to the ship's doctor that it wasn't my heart. I just couldn't breathe, but he kept insisting I needed to see a heart doctor. Feeling I might not get the proper treatment, we chose not to go to that hospital, so the ship's concierge booked us a flight home at the small airport in Huatulco.

We left the ship at Huatulco, went through Customs, and took a cab through the city, trying to get to the airport. Unfortunately, the cab got to an area where we couldn't get around some school children who were picketing with their parents because they were tired of the school system. It must have been a private school, because the children were wearing uniforms.

We were on the only road to the airport, and there was no way the cab driver could get around the crowd. He said we would have to get out and walk across the bridge, which would take us beyond the crowd. Virginia explained to the driver that I was in no shape to be walking anywhere, which I wasn't. Unfortunately, we didn't have a choice. We had to get out of the cab and walk around the crowd and across the bridge, while pulling our luggage on wheels behind us. And we only had an hour left to get on the plane.

The cab driver called his cousin, and the cousin met us on the other side of the bridge in his cab and drove us to the airport. We'd paid the first cab driver, but the cousin cab driver wouldn't let us pay him. He said his cousin would pay him. Both nice fellows.

The airport held the plane for us as well as for some other people who'd had trouble getting to the airport, or we would have missed our flight—the only flight for that day. From there we flew to Mexico City, where we had to buy visas (cash only) to leave the country, then we flew home to Houston.

Fortunately, we'd bought insurance for the cruise, just in case, so we recouped all the money we'd spent on that trip, except for $5.40 for a sandwich at the airport.

When we got back home, I went to the doctor and was diagnosed with chronic obstructive pulmonary disease (COPD), for which I now take medication.

90 Years Young

On Saturday, August 31, 2013, Virginia surprised me with a 90th birthday party in the Fellowship Hall at the Northwest 4SQ Life Church. The place was packed with family members and long-time friends.

L-R: Joe Carl III; Joe Carl, Jr.; Jerry

Hurricane Harvey ~ August 2017

> *Harvey was the strongest landfall in this area, known as the Texas Coastal Bend, since Hurricane Carla in September 1961.*
>
> *Harvey's extreme slow movement Aug. 26-30, 2017, resulted in catastrophic flooding.*
>
> *Harvey's flooding caused one of the worst weather disasters in U.S. history, with a price tag that would amount to billions of dollars. It was estimated that 70% of Harris County was flooded by at least 1.5 feet of water, with an estimated 136,000 flooded structures in the county alone, as of August 31.*
>
> *Thousands of water rescues occurred in the Houston metro area as many homes and businesses were swamped by floodwaters.*
>
> *~ https://weather.com/storms/hurricane/news/tropical-storm-harvey-forecast-texas-louisiana-arkansas*

Like many other homes, our home flooded as well. Fortunately, Virginia had made sure we had flood insurance, since one of her previous homes had flooded years ago. And, while many material things were lost, Virginia and I are still here, with everything either repaired or replaced.

Then, during Valentine Week of 2021, Texas was under a winter storm warning, with extremely cold temperatures and blanketed with snow, sleet, and freezing rain, causing power outages that lasted for several days. Fortunately, we have a gas fireplace, so we were warm and cozy.

Chapter 20

When it's over, it's not who we were,
it's whether we made a difference.
~ Unknown

Flyers, Reunions, Good-Byes

Hollywood Stars Who Served in the USAAF in WWII

~ https://www.thevintagenews.com/2016/05/05/
top-10-hollywood-stars-served-wwii/

Immediately after the Japanese attacked the U.S. Naval Base at Pearl Harbor, killing more than 2,400 people and destroying a considerable number of battleships and planes, the entire nation joined the war effort in some way. Actors were no different.

Here are a few famous names you may recognize who served in the United States Army Air Forces at the same time I did.

Charles Bronson made a name for himself by playing tough-guy and anti-hero roles. But he had proved that he was a real-life tough guy years before he appeared as one on the big screen. The legendary actor, who starred as Henry Fonda's nemesis in Sergio Leone's classic *Once Upon a Time in the West* and as the anti-hero in *Death Wish*, enlisted in the United States Army Air Forces in 1943 and served as a tail gunner.

He was five feet nine inches tall, which made him perfect for arguably the most dangerous combat position: tail gunner. Stuck in the rear end of the aircraft, tail gunners had a slim chance of survival, and it is no wonder that this assignment in World War II had the highest casualty rates.

However, Bronson managed to survive the "airman's coffin," taking part in 25 missions and receiving a Purple Heart when World War II came to an end.

Charlton Heston joined the military in 1944 at the age of 21 and served two years as a radio operator and aerial gunner on a B-25 Mitchell.

The man who earned the Academy Award for Best Actor for his portrayal of Judah Ben-Hur in William Wyler's epic *Ben-Hur* and starred as Moses in Cecil B. DeMille's *The Ten Commandments* reached the rank of Staff Sergeant during World War II.

Although Heston never saw combat because he was stationed in the Alaskan Aleutian Islands, after becoming a Hollywood star he was asked by the military to narrate some highly classified military films about nuclear weapons. This task required him to hold the nation's highest security clearance level, known as "Q clearance," for six years.

Unlike Bronson and Heston, **James "Jimmy" Stewart** had already appeared in a number of movies, including *You Can't Take It With You*, *Mr. Smith Goes to Washington*, and *Destry Rides Again*, before he enlisted in the military.

Coming from a family with a tradition of service in the Army, Stewart was destined to have a fascinating military career. He was a flying enthusiast and had already earned his private pilot certificate in 1935. However, when he tried to enlist in the U.S. Army in 1940, he was rejected for failing to meet the weight requirement for his height.

That's when he sought the help of MGM's muscle man and trainer, Don Loomis. By March 1941, Stewart successfully enlisted with the Army Air Corps and spent the next nine months at Moffett Field, California, where he received his basic training.

In January 1942, he was commissioned as a Second Lieutenant and served as a four-engine instructor at Moffett Field before he was eventually sent overseas. Stewart took part in 20 important combat missions, and, by the end of the war, he had risen to the rank of Colonel. He was awarded the Distinguished Flying Cross with two Oak Leaf Clusters, the Air Medal with three Oak Leaf Clusters, and the French Croix de Guerre with Palm. Stewart continued to play a role in the Army Air Forces Reserve following World War II and the new United States Air Force Reserve after the official establishment of the Air Force as an independent service in 1947. On July 23, 1959, Stewart was promoted to Brigadier General. During his active-duty periods, he remained current as a pilot of various jets and bombers of the Strategic Air Command.

After 27 years of service, Stewart officially retired from the Air Force on May 31, 1968, and was awarded the United States Air Force Distinguished Service Medal. On May 23, 1985, President Ronald Reagan awarded Stewart the Presidential Medal of Freedom, simultaneously advancing Stewart to the rank of Major General on the U.S. Air Force Retired list.

Widely known as Uncle Fester from the 1960s sitcom "The Addams Family," **Jackie Coogan** is also considered the first major child star in American movie history. But what is less well known about him is that he took part in the war effort, enlisting in the Army before the United States had officially entered the war.

Following the Japanese attack on December 7, 1941, Coogan requested a transfer to the Army Air Force as he was an experienced civilian pilot. Upon graduation from glider school, he was made a flight officer and soon participated in a very dangerous mission.

In March 1944, Coogan was among the glider pilots who took part in a mission in Burma known as Operation Broadway. On March 5, 1944, he flew some of Orde Wingate's Chindits into Burma and helped the Allies establish a foothold behind Japanese lines.

While attending Joplin High School (Missouri), **Robert "Bob" Cummings** was taught to fly by his godfather, Orville Wright, the aviation pioneer. His first solo was on March 3, 1927. During his high school years, Cummings gave Joplin residents rides in his aircraft for $5 per person. When the government began licensing flight instructors, Cummings was issued

Flight Instructor Certificate No. 1, making him the first official flight instructor in the United States.

In November 1942, Cummings joined the United States Army Air Forces. During World War II, he served as a flight instructor. After the war, Cummings served as a pilot in the United States Air Force Reserve, where he achieved the rank of Captain.

During his Hollywood years, he appeared in 68 films, one of which was Alfred Hitchcock's *Dial M for Murder*. He also appeared in 24 television shows, including his own "The Bob Cummings Show" from 1955 to 1959.

Perhaps the biggest of the Hollywood stars who joined the Armed Forces was "the King of Hollywood," **Clark Gable**.

Emotionally and physically devastated after his beloved wife Carole Lombard (who was selling war bonds) died in a plane crash, joining the Army seemed to be the only thing that could rally his spirits. So, he sent a telegram to President Franklin D. Roosevelt asking for a role in the war effort.

Gable enlisted in the U.S. Army Air Corps on August 12, 1942, as a gunner, and, after completing the 13-week training, he was commissioned as a Second Lieutenant. Although Gable was 40 years old when he enlisted as a private in the Army Air Corps, he participated in many high-profile combat missions during the war with the Eighth Air Force (91st Bomb Group) in England.

The Germans considered the famous actor enemy number one and made several unsuccessful attempts to capture him alive. Reportedly, Adolf Hitler, who was one of Gable's greatest fans, offered a $5,000 reward to anyone who could capture Clark Gable and bring him to Germany.

Hitler's plan to capture Gable proved to be unsuccessful, and the actor returned to the United States safe and sound. For his heroic service, he was awarded the Air Medal, the Distinguished Flying Cross, American Campaign Medal, European-African-Middle Eastern Campaign Medal, and World War II Victory Medal.

100th Bomb Group Reunions

The other day I [Bill Carleton] came across my "pocket mission report" for the 351st Squadron, dated September 29, 1944, to April 27, 1945.

Within two hours after each mission, Squadron Engineering would report to Group Operations the status of each plane. Operations had a large board showing the individual status of the entire group. This information was vital for the mission they were then planning for the next day.

Usually by midnight, Squadron Engineering would be advised as to the next effort and which planes would be involved. We would then load these planes with the specified amount of fuel, and ordnance would hang the correct number and type of bombs. Also placed on board was the ammunition, oxygen, communications, and other special details. The crew chief would then pre-flight the plane. As dawn broke, our final gesture would be topping off the fuel tanks to replace the gas used for the pre-flight. As the Madam said, "We are open 24 hours a day, but mostly at night."

~ https://100thbg.com/ (Splasher 6 Newsletter, Fall 2006, "Gentlemen, Start Your Engines" article by Bill Carleton)

It's interesting the things you remember as you go back over your life, especially at a reunion of men you knew during the war, particularly the men you flew with.

The first reunion Evelyn and I attended was in 1978 in Long Beach, California, held aboard the RMS *Queen Mary*. The last time I had seen the *Queen Mary* was in January 1945 while aboard the SS *Île de France,* the ship on which my crew and I had crossed the Atlantic to Scotland. The *Queen Mary* was now a floating hotel.

It was the place where I met up with Hank Cervantes (copilot), Paul Gerling (tail gunner), Norman Larsen (radio operator/gunner), and Tony Picone (navigator), whom I hadn't seen since the end of the war when all the troops were sent home. It was great to see them again.

I wasn't able to make all the reunions, and I'm not in many of the photos taken at the reunions I was able to attend, but here are a few photos of those moments.

Long Beach, CA 1987: L-R: Fran Larsen; Henry "Hank" Cervantes; Norman Larsen; Rose Picone; Tony Picone; Evelyn Martin; Joe C. Martin, Jr. Rose & Tony Picone are holding an original A-2 jacket, "Miss Temptation." ~ https://100thbg.com/ (Photo Gallery)

Long Beach, CA 1987:
L-R: Fran Larsen; Barbara Gerling; Henry "Hank" Cervantes; Paul Gerling; Joe Carl Martin, Jr.; Evelyn Martin; Norman Larsen ~ Personal Photo

Pittsburgh, PA 2005: L-R: Paul Gerling; Joe Carl Martin, Jr.; Henry "Hank" Cervantes; Joe Carl Martin III ~ Personal Photo

Pittsburgh, PA 2005: L-R: Jerry Martin; Virginia Martin; Janice Martin; Joe Carl Martin, Jr.; Dante

Savannah, GA 2013: 100th Bomb Group Vets in front of the WWII *Memphis Belle* (Movie) B-17 at the Hunter Army Air Field. Joe Carl Martin, Jr., is standing 7th man from the left in the short sleeved

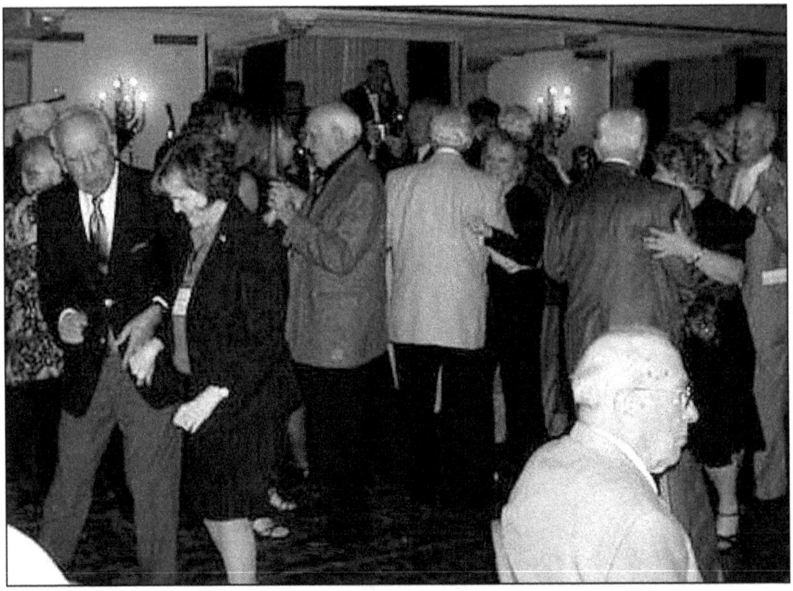

Pittsburgh, PA 2005: Henry “Hank” Cervantes jitterbugging with my daughter-in-law Janice, and that’s me and Virginia (short-sleeve, dark dress) to the far right. We were dancing to Glenn Miller’s “In The Mood.” ~ Personal Photo

Dallas, TX 2021: L-R: Jerry Martin; Henry “Hank” Cervantes; Joe Carl Martin, III ~ Personal Photo – 100th Bomb Group Reunion

TAPS

1st Lt. Joe Carl Martin, Jr., Crew
349th Bomb Squadron of the 100th Bomb Group
Thorpe Abbotts Air Base, England

Alfred S. Collins, March 11, 1922 to December 13, 1971, North Carolina

- Ball Turret Gunner, Cpl. Alfred S. Collins (He replaced Sgt. Celeste "Les" Rossi.)

William E. Dudecz, September 16, 1923 to August 23, 1991, Connecticut

- Top Turret Gunner/Engineer, T/Sgt. William "Dude" E. Dudecz

Paul R. Gerling, August 15, 1925 to August 27, 2016, New York

- Tail Gunner, S/Sgt. Paul Gerling

Norman E. Larsen, December 25, 1924 to March 29, 1999, Washington

- Radio Operator/Gunner, Sgt. Norman Larsen

Antonio S. Picone, August 19, 1918 to June 26, 1996, Michigan

- Navigator, 2nd Lt. Antonio "Tony" Picone

Celeste "Les" Rossi, January 10, 1923 to January 27, 2016, Florida

- Ball Turret Gunner, Sgt. Celeste "Les" Rossi (He transferred out of our crew after a few missions. Rossi received an offer to learn how to operate a new type radar used to scramble the radar on anti-aircraft guns.)

Matthew "Matt" Schipper, April 24, 1917 to August 25, 1973, Michigan

- Waist Gunner, S/Sgt. Matthew "Matt" Schipper (the oldest man on the crew, age 28)

Ralph E. Spada, October 16, 1925 to April 25, 2000, Ohio

- Togglier(Bombardier)/Nose Gunner, S/Sgt. Ralph Spada (From his position in the Plexiglas nose of the plane, Spada had a switch to open the bomb bay doors and a toggle switch to release the bombs.)

As of the publication of this book, **Henry "Hank" Cervantes**, former Warrant Officer and my copilot, is alive and well and living in California.

As a Second Lieutenant at the end of the war, Hank remained in the United States Army Air Forces, making the transition from the USAAF to the United States Air Force. Initially part of the United States Army, the USAF was formed as a separate branch of the military on September 18, 1947.

Hank went on to become a jet pilot with the Strategic Air Command and retired in 1965 as a Lieutenant Colonel. You can read more about his story in his book, *Piloto: Migrant Worker to Jet Pilot.*

WWII Aircraft Boneyard

✈ ✈ ✈

The following excerpt is from *Piloto: Migrant Worker To Jet Pilot,* © 2007 (110-112) by Lt. Col. Henry Cervantes, USAF (Ret.) and my former copilot "Hank." It is quoted here with his permission.

"I volunteered to ferry war-weary B-17s from Plains Field at Lubbock, Texas, to Kingman Field, Arizona. Thousands of bomber crewmen had trained at the former gunnery school, but it was now a collection point for Air Corps aircraft on their way to auction, a smelter, or the scrap heap.

"At one time, more than 7,000 planes, most of them flyable, were parked on the desert floor southeast of the airfield. The armada included 1,832 B-17s, 2,562 B-24s, 478 P-38s, and hundreds of P-47s. B-17s sold for $13,750, although some sold for as little as $750. Most Mustangs and Thunderbolts went for $3,500, P-40 Warhawks for $1,250. One fellow bought 5,437 planes for less than $3 million.

"One day I borrowed a jeep and, determined to find *E-Z Goin'*, went to the B-17 parking area. From a distance, the fleet appeared to be seaplanes floating on shimmering heat waves. Up close, they no longer bore any semblance to the powerful juggernauts that had beaten the Luftwaffe's best in vicious air battles, proven the case for daylight bombing, and brought Germany to its knees. Gone were the aircrews with their flight-kits, yellow Mae-Wests, and parachutes. Gone were the ground crewmen in greasy sheepskin jackets, dirty fatigues, and floppy caps. And gone were the fuel or oil trucks, tugs, bomb trailers, hardstands, and maintenance tents. All that remained was an armada of old war-horses silently living out their last days hunched against a fiery wind. Many were cannibalized or half-deconstructed with nothing more to manifest their days of glory than a faded array of designs, circles, stripes, bars, insignias, and catchy names. Once badges of honor, the markings now seemed no more meaningful than a child's art displayed on a refrigerator door.

"After an hour of bouncing in and out of gopher holes, I spotted the 100th's block combat markings and *E-Z Goin'*s nose art. Her paint had peeled, a tire was flat, the engine nacelles were clogged with tumbleweeds, and the flight control surfaces were flapping in the breeze. I greeted her as one would a sick friend. 'Hi,' I said, 'they're not treating you very well here.' I circled her slowly like a mother inspecting a child, patting her here and wiping a smudge there. Inside, the fuselage was like an abandoned roaster oven. Dust, dirt, and cobwebs were everywhere. I squeezed through the bomb bay to the flight deck. My two long, emergency yellow, USAAF, back-cushions were still in place, and a cloud of dust rose when I sat down. Rather than months, it seemed like years since I had sat in my confessional and prayed the fervent prayers that all airmen pray at one time or another.

"Time came to leave. I closed my eyes and thanked *E-Z Goin'* for all the times she brought me home, even when I had little faith she could. I locked the flight controls, returned the levers, switches, and knobs to off, and closed the windows and doors. Although she had fallen on hard times, to me she was still a battle-tested friend and a proud member of the Bloody 100th. As I drove away, I avoided looking into the rearview mirror. I wanted to remember her as she had been in her glory days as a mighty Flying Fortress."

~ https://pixels.com/featured/vintage-b-17-cockpit-mike-burgquist.html

We
Are
The

Kingman Army Air Field After World War II
~ https://www.airplaneboneyards.com/kingman-arizona-airplane-boneyard-storage.htm

100th

When Friendship, Love, and Truth
Abound among a band of brothers,
The cup of joy goes gaily round.
Each shares the bliss of others.
Sweet roses grace the thorny way,
Along the wall of sorrow.
The flowers that shed their leaves today
Shall bloom again tomorrow.
How grand in age, how fair in youth
Are holy Friendship, Love, and Truth.

~ From an English Jug, circa 1820

Chapter 21

This is my story, this is my song, praising my Savior all the day long.
"Blessed Assurance" ~ Fanny J. Crosby

Final Thoughts
(2017)

In these quiet days of my senior years, I get around with the help of a pacemaker and a walker. Bad knees and back problems have slowed me down a might. Some memories have faded away.

Of course, my children are grown with grandchildren of their own—my great grandchildren. What a blessing to be able to watch them all grow up.

My first-born son Joe Carl III is happily married to his wife Suzanne, who has two children from her first marriage—Joey, a former Marine, and Melissa. Both her children are married and have children of their own. Joe Carl III has two children from his first marriage—Dante and Heather. Dante has two sons with his wife Terrie—Dante Sebastian and Owen. Heather is raising her son Nicholas in Wyoming.

My second-born son Jerry has been happily married to his wife Janice for 50 years and counting. They have two children—Jerry, Jr., and Jennifer. Jerry, Jr., and his wife Cristina have three children—Payton, Brandon, and Sophie. Jennifer and her husband Kevin have one son, Gavin.

My two foster daughters—Darline (who passed away from liver cancer in 2016) and Linda came to live with Evelyn and me when they were toddlers. They called us Mother and Daddy, and their children call me Pawpaw, the same as my other grandchildren and great grandchildren.

God has blessed me in many ways, particularly, with the love of two wives—Evelyn for almost 52 years (who passed away from ovarian cancer in 1994) and Virginia for 20 years and counting.

Yes, it's been a good life, and as I finish this final chapter, one thought remains above all else . . . God's hand is still on my shoulder.

Post Script

Former 1st Lt. Joe Carl Martin, Jr., is now in God's hands. He departed to be face to face with the Lord on September 28, 2021, at the age of 98. He was laid to rest in Houston National Cemetery following a 21-gun salute and a trumpeter who played "Taps."

Virginia Hetzel Martin departed to be face to face with the Lord on February 3, 2022, at the age of 79. She was laid to rest next to Carl.

October 3, 2021: American flag flown at half-mast at Thorpe Abbotts, England, in honor of former 1st Lt Joe Carl Martin, Jr. Photo courtesy of Ron and Carol Batley and made possible with the assistance of Matt Mabe and the Board of Directors, 100th Bomb Group Foundation.

Distinguished Flying Cross Citation

For extraordinary achievement while participating in a bombing mission over Buchen, Germany, on 7 April 1945. 1st Lt. Joe Martin's B-17 bomber was attacked by an enemy plane. The left horizontal stabilizer and elevator were torn away, top half of the tail and rudder sliced off, the fuselage cut approximately through 2/3 of its thickness, and bullet holes in the left side of the nose. With the number one engine trailing smoke and the autopilot, radio, and intercom disabled, Lt. Martin held the plane in formation and successfully dropped the payload of bombs on the designated target. Unable to gain altitude with the rest of the squadron, Lt. Martin had no choice but to drop out of formation, fly through unceasing flak, while continuing to lose altitude as they headed back to their home base in England and landing without further damage to crew or plane. The courage and professional skill shown by Lt. Martin in performing a seemingly impossible feat reflects great credit upon himself and the United States Army Air Forces.

100th Bomb Group Abbreviated History

By Harry Crosby, Jan Ridding, and Michael Faley

(Complete History may be found at https://100thbg.com/)

The "Hundredth Bombardment Group" came into being "on paper" at Orlando Army Base, Florida, on June 1, 1942. It would not be until October 27, 1942, in Boise, Idaho, by "Special Order 300," that 230 enlisted men and 24 officers were transferred to the 100th. The group was officially activated on November 14, 1942, when Col. Darr Alkire became the group's first Commanding Officer. In December, during their second phase of training, the total strength of the Group was 37 crews, with ten men on each crew. At that time, Capt. John Egan was Operations Officer with Capt. William Veal, 349th Bomb Squadron Commanding Officer (BS C.O.); Capt. Gale "Buck" Cleven, 350th BS C.O.; Capt. John "Jack" Kidd, 351st BS C.O.; and Capt. Robert Flesher, 418th BS C.O.

The 100th Bomb Group trained at Walla Walla, Washington; Wendover Field, Utah; Sioux City, Iowa; and Kearney, Nebraska. It was at Kearny on April 20, 1943, that all 37 original crews took off on a practice mission for Hamilton Field, California, a distance of almost 1,300 miles with very poor results. Col. Alkire shouldered this responsibility and was relieved of command of the 100th BG and assigned weeks later as Commanding Officer of the 449th Bomb Group (B-24's), which would later fly with the 15th Air Force out of Italy.

On April 26, 1943, Col. Howard Turner, assumed command of the Group, and, on May 1, the air echelon took off for Wendover Field, Utah, for 20 days of advanced training in navigation, gunnery, bombing, and formation flying, while aircraft combat modifications were being done at Ogden, Utah. With training completed, 35 crews flew to England on May 25, 1943, and arrived at Station 139, Thorpe Abbotts, England, on June 8, 1943. Three days later, Col. Turner was assigned to the First Air Division and was replaced by Col. Harold Huglin, who made the following changes: Maj. Egan to 418th BS C.O., Capt. Flesher to Air Exec, Capt. Kidd to Operations Officer, and Capt. Ollie Turner to 351st BS C.O.

The 100th Bomb Group (H), flying the B-17 "Flying Fortress," would become combat operational beginning June 25, 1943. Any sense of adventure and bravado came to a halt on that first mission. Three planes and 30 men were lost over Bremen. The average life of an 8th Air Force B-17 crewman in 1943 was eleven missions! On July 2, 1943, Col. Neil B. "Chick" Harding assumed command of the 100th BG, with Col. Huglin being reassigned to 13th Combat Wing HQ. "Chick" would command the 100th until March 7, 1944, and, by that time, the group had already become legendary.

From June 25, 1943, until April 20, 1945, the 100th Bomb Group would never go off operational status due to losses. The 100th did not stand alone at Thorpe Abbotts. Throughout their stay, they were assisted by the following support units: 1776 Ordnance Company, 18th Weather Detachment, 869th Chemical Company, 216th Finance Section, 592nd Postal Unit, 1285th Military Police, 2110th Fire Fighting Platoon, 1141st Quartermaster Company, 83rd Service Group, 456th Sub-Depot, 412th Air Service Group, 838th Air Engineering Squadron, 662nd Air Material Squadron, American Red Cross, and Royal Air Force Detachment. Throughout its stay at Thorpe Abbotts, the Ground Echelon of the 100th was cited frequently for its excellent maintenance and preparation activity.

Combat Narrative:

The 100th Bomb Group, from June 1943 to January 1944, concentrated its efforts against airfields, submarine facilities, and aircraft industries in occupied France and Germany. During this time, the Group was involved in the epic air battles over Regensburg on August 17, 1943 (for which it received its first Presidential Unit Citation) and Black Week—October 8-14, 1943 (Bremen, Munster, Marienburg, and Schweinfurt—nicknamed "Black Thursday" because the 8th Air Force lost 60 bombers). It led the bombing of Rujkan, Norway, which delayed the manufacture of heavy water for the German atomic bomb.

January through May 1944, the Group bombed enemy airfields, industries, marshalling yards, and V-1 missile sites, including participation in the Allied campaign against enemy aircraft factories during Big Week—February 20-25, 1944. The Group participated in the first daylight raid against Berlin (March 4, 1944) and completed a series of attacks against Berlin on March 6 and 8, 1944, for which the 100th Bomb Group was awarded a second Presidential Unit Citation (also called the Distinguished Unit Citation). During this time, the Group suffered the loss of their beloved Col. Harding who was relieved of command due to illness, and his replacement, Col. Robert H. Kelly, was shot down on his first mission on April 28, 1944, one week after taking command.

In the summer of 1944, oil installations became the major target. The Group also engaged in support and interdictory missions, hitting bridges and gun positions in preparation for the Normandy Invasion in June 1944. On June 6, 1944, D-Day, the Group flew three missions in support of the ground troops. Later that month, the 100th participated in the First Russian Shuttle Mission, led by new Group C.O. Col. Thomas S. Jeffrey.

July through September 1944 saw the 100th BG strike at enemy positions in St. Lo and Brest and concentrated on the oil refineries at Merseburg, Ruhland, Politz, and Hamburg. They flew a Second Russian Shuttle Mission along with two low-level supply drops to the French Maquis. The 100th Bomb Group received the French Croix de Guerre with Palm for attacking heavily defended German installations and for dropping supplies to the French Forces of the Interior.

In October through December 1944, the Century Bombers attacked transportation, oil refineries, and ground defenses in the drive against the Siegfried Line. They were involved in the December 24, 1944, mission to attack communication centers and airfields in the Ardennes sector during the Battle of the Bulge.

On February 2, 1945, Col. Frederick J. Sutterlin took command of the 100th Bomb Group and would remain there until after the end of the War. On February 3, 1945, the 100th Bomb Group led the entire Third Air Division on a mission to "Big B" (Berlin). Leading the group was Maj. Robert "Rosie" Rosenthal flying his 52nd Mission.

January to April 1945, the Group concentrated on marshalling yards, bridges, factories, docks, oil refineries, and ground support (including the airborne assault across the Rhine in March 1945). By March 1945, the Luftwaffe was a limited but effective force and used both ME 262 jet fighters and ramming techniques (April 7, 1945, Büchen mission) to try to thwart the 100th Bomb Group and the 8th Air Force's continual bombing. On April 20, 1945, the 100th Bomb Group flew its last combat mission to Oranienburg (Berlin) with no losses.

Statistical Summary:

First mission: June 25, 1943
Last mission: April 20, 1945
Total missions: 306
Total credit sorties: 8,630
Total bomb tonnage: 19,257
Missing Air Crew Reports: 184
Planes Lost or Salvaged: 229
KIA/MIA: 768 men and POW: 939 men
"Chowhound" missions: 6 in May 1945
(dropping food to hungry Dutch citizens)

Campaign Credits:

1. Air Offensive, Europe (4 July 1942 – 5 June 1944)
2. Normandy (6 June 1944 – 24 July 1944)
3. Northern France (25 July 1944 – 14 September 1944)
4. Rhineland (15 September 1944 – 21 March 1945)
5. Ardennes - Alsace (16 December 1944 – 25 January 1945)
6. Central Europe (22 March 1945 – 11 May 1945)

Awards and Decorations:

Two Presidential Unit Citations:

1. Regensburg, Germany – August 17, 1943
2. Berlin, Germany – March 4, 6, 8, 1944

French Croix de Guerre with Palm: June 25 – December 31, 1944

Commanding Officers	**Dates**
Col. Darr H. Alkire	14 Nov 1942 – 25 Apr 1943
Col. Howard M. Turner	26 Apr 1943 – 10 Jun 1943
Col. Harold Q. Huglin	11 Jun 1943 – 01 Jul 1943
Col. Neil B. "Chick" Harding	02 Jul 1943 – 06 Mar 1944

Lt Col. John Bennett, temporary CO............07 Mar 1944 – 19 Apr 1944
Col. Robert H. Kelly..................................... 20 Apr 1944 – 28 Apr 1944
Lt Col. John Bennett, temporary CO........... 29 Apr 1944 – 06 May 1944
Col. Thomas Jeffrey ....07 May 1944 – 01 Feb 1945
Col. Frederick Sutterlin .... 02 Feb 1945 – 23 Jun 1945
Col. John Wallace.. 24 Jun 1945 – 01 Aug 1945
Col. Harry F. Cruver..01 Aug 1945 – Dec 1945

Although the 100th did not have the highest over-all loss rate of any group in the Eighth Air Force, it did have heavy losses during eight missions to Germany, thus, earning the nickname **"The Bloody Hundredth."**

Date	**Aircraft Lost**
17 Aug 1943	Nine aircraft lost at Regensburg
08 Oct 1943	Seven aircraft lost at Bremen
10 Oct 1943	Twelve aircraft lost at Munster
06 Mar 1944	Fifteen aircraft lost at Berlin
24 May 1944	Nine aircraft lost at Berlin
29 July 1944	Eight aircraft lost at Merseburg
11 Sep 1944	Twelve aircraft lost at Ruhland
31 Dec 1944	Twelve aircraft lost at Hamburg

100th Bomb Group Patches

100th Bomb Group - Official

100th BG – Unofficial
Worn 1944-45

349th Bomb Squadron

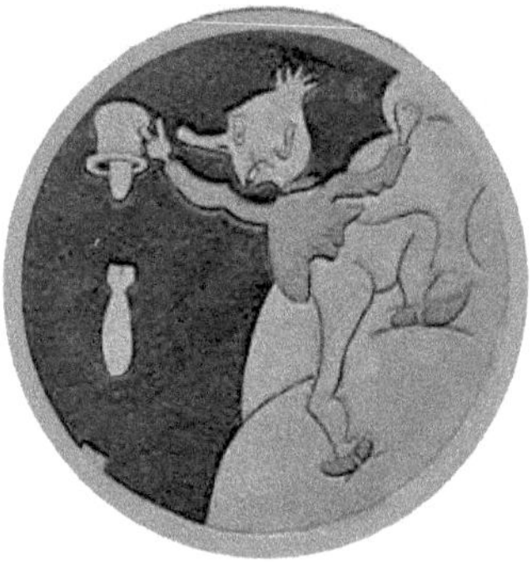

350th Bomb Squadron

351st Bomb Squadron

418th Bomb Squadron

Bibliography

Personal Notes and Recorded Recollections of Joe Carl Martin, Jr.

Books

- Cervantes, Henry, Lt. Col. USAF (Ret.). *Piloto: Migrant Worker to Jet Pilot.* Henry Cervantes, 2007.
- Jablonski, Edward. *Flying Fortress: The Illustrated Biography of the B-17s and the Men Who Flew Them*. Garden City, New York: Doubleday & Company, Inc., 1965.
- John R. Reagan High School, *The Pennant, 1942* (yearbook) Houston, Texas
- Le Strange, Richard (Assisted by James R. Brown). *Century Bombers: The Story of the Bloody Hundredth*. England: 100th Bomb Group Memorial Museum, Thorpe Abbotts, 1989.
- Miller, Donald L. *Masters of the Air*. New York: Simon & Schuster Paperbacks, 2006.
- Roush, Jr., Colonel John H. *World War II Reminiscences.* Colonel John H. Roush, Jr., 2013.
- Walker, John H. and Wingate, Gwendolyn. *Beaumont, A Pictorial History*. Virginia: The Donning Company/Publishers, 1983.
- Wiesel, Elie. *Night.* New York: Hill and Wang, 1972, 1985; Translation 2006 by Marion Wiesel.

Articles

- https://www.britannica.com/event/Great-Depression
- http://png.high.schoolfusion.us/modules/groups/homepagefiles/cms/446867/File/history.pdf?sessionid=37b97981363e5b4d7b5458e6db20d19f: *Port Neches Independent School District (16-page document)*
- http://www.thc.texas.gov/public/upload/publications/tx-in-wwII.pdf: *Texas Historical Commission – Texas in World War II (24-page document)*
- https://today.ttu.edu/posts/2015/08/wwii-saved-united-states-and-texas-tech: *World War II Saved United States and Texas Tech*
- http://www.hobbsnm.org/files/engineering/planning/haaf_history.pdf: *The Hobbs Army Air Field: Its History & Archaeology (124-page document)*
- http://www.hobbshistory.com/HAAFYearbook/index.html: *Hobbs Army Air Field Yearbook 1943 –Images of the men and women who trained and served at the Army Air Force base in Hobbs, New Mexico. (Web Album Generator)*
- https://ww2.stripes.com/epaper/special-publications/wasp: *Stars and Stripes Salutes Women Airforce Service Pilots (16-page document)*
- Wolders, Robert. "The Real Audrey" (article). *People* magazine, August 28, 2017 (excerpt from page 46).
- https://historycollection.jsc.nasa.gov/JSCHistoryPortal/history/ellington/Ellington.pdf (60-page document published in 1999)
- https://100thbg.com/ (*Splasher 6 Newsletter*, Fall 2006, "Gentlemen, Start Your Engines" article by Bill Carleton)

Websites

I used quite a bit of information and a few photos that I found on Wikipedia. In many cases, there were links to actual sites where Wikipedia had found their information and photos; therefore, I was able to verify the information that you will find throughout this book. JEM

- https://en.wikipedia.org/wiki/Spindletop: *Spindletop is a salt dome oil field located in the southern portion of Beaumont, Texas in the United States.*
- https://www.lamar.edu/spindletop-gladys-city/spindletop-history.html
- https://en.wikipedia.org/wiki/Shongaloo,_Louisiana
- https://www.hotsprings.org/pages/history-buffs/: *Fun and popular spots in Hot Springs for history buffs.*
- https://marlintx.net/about/: *Marlin, Texas – City History*
- https://abc13.com/when-it-snowed-in-houston-historic-snowstorm-snow-film/1197144/
- https://www.sinclairoil.com/history/1930.html: *When the Great Depression hit, Mr. Sinclair made the boldest gamble of his life.*
- https://en.wikipedia.org/wiki/Sinclair_Oil_Corporation: *Sinclair Oil Corporation is an American petroleum corporation, founded by Harry F. Sinclair on May 1, 1916 . . .*
- https://www.weather.gov/fwd/1929snow: *Historic Texas Snowstorm: December 20-21, 1929*
- https://en.wikipedia.org/wiki/Pirogue: *A type of boat associated particularly with the Cajuns of the Louisiana marsh.*
- https://www.houstonpress.com/news/woodwind-lakes-subdivision-built-on-oil-and-gas-field-turns-on-neighbor-who-pointed-out-the-contamination-6574095
- https://tshaonline.org/handbook/online/articles/hvf03: *Texas State Historical Association – Fairbanks, Texas*
- https://www.tshaonline.org/handbook/entries/oil-and-gas-industry
- http://www.nationalww2museum.org/learn/education/for-students/ww2-history/take-a-closer-look/ration-books.html?referrer=https://www.google.com/: *The National WWII Museum, New Orleans, Louisiana – Ration Books*
- https://upload.wikimedia.org/wikipedia/commons/f/f3/%22This_Store_is_pledged_to_conform_to_the_Sugar_Regulations_of_the_Food_Administration._Your_Sugar_Ration_is_2lbs._per_mo_-_NARA_-_512525.jpg: *Ration Coupon Photo*
- https://en.wikipedia.org/wiki/Attack_on_Pearl_Harbor

- https://www.gsa.gov/portal/ext/html/site/hb/category/25431/actionParameter/exploreByBuilding/buildingId/11: *U.S. Custom House, Houston, Texas*
- https://en.wikipedia.org/wiki/United_States_Customhouse_(Houston): *The United States Customhouse is a historic custom house located at Houston in Harris County, Texas (with photo).*
- https://100thbg.com/: *Official Website of the 100th Bomb Group (Heavy) Foundation*
- https://100thbg.com/index.php?option=com_content&view=article&id=28&Itemid=174&gallery=19&limitstart=216: *Home > Galleries > Photos > 349th Bomb Squadron*
- http://www.mybaseguide.com/air_force/36-128/sheppard_afb_history: *Sheppard Air Force Base - History*
- https://en.wikipedia.org/wiki/Texas_World_War_II_Army_Airfields: *Texas World War II Army Airfields*
- http://www.astrosdaily.com/history/houstonunionstation/: *Houston Union Station: The Great Hall Revealed by Tom Marsh*
- https://en.wikipedia.org/wiki/Union_Station_(Houston): *Union Station (Houston)*
- https://www.youtube.com/watch?v=hBX1zsrk14E: *CHAPTER 03 Houston's Union Station and Railroads, Minute Maid Park*
- https://www.costamesahistory.org/learn/saaab.htm: *Costa Mesa Historical Society – Santa Ana Army Air Base*
- http://www.stearman.at/boeing_stearman.html: *History of The Boeing Stearman Aircraft*
- https://www.tularehistoricalmuseum.org/rankin.html: *Tulare History – Rankin Field*
- https://www.wmof.com/bt-13.html: *Western Museum of Flight – Vultee BT-13 Valiant*
- https://www.militarymuseum.org/CastleAFB.html: *Historic California Posts, Camps, Stations and Airfields – Castle Air Force Base – (Air Corps Basic Flying School-Merced, Merced Army Air Field, Castle Field)*

- https://en.wikipedia.org/wiki/Marfa,_Texas: *Marfa is a city in the high desert of the Trans-Pecos in far West Texas . . .*
- https://en.wikipedia.org/wiki/Marfa_Army_Air_Field: *During World War II, Marfa Army Airfield was an installation of the Army Air Force Training Command West Coast Training Center.*
- https://en.wikipedia.org/wiki/Amarillo_Air_Force_Base: *Amarillo Air Force Base, originally Amarillo Army Air Field is a former United States Air Force base located in Potter County, Texas . . .*
- http://waspmuseum.org/: *National WASP World War II Museum – Avenger Field, Sweetwater, Texas*
- http://www.nationalmuseum.af.mil/Visit/Museum-Exhibits/Fact-Sheets/Display/Article/196418/brig-gen-william-billy-mitchell/: *National Museum of the U.S. Air Force – Brig. Gen. William "Billy" Mitchell*
- http://www.aviation-history.com/boeing/b17.html: *The Aviation History Online Museum – Boeing B-17 Flying Fortress*
- http://www.303rdbg.com/crew-duties.html: *Hell's Angels: 303rd Bomb Group (H) - Duties and Responsibilities of The Airplane Commander, from the B-17 Pilot Training Manual -1943*
- http://cdn.toptenreviews.com/rev/prod/ce/57244-revell-b17-flying-fortress-box.jpg: *B-17 Flying Fortress Photo*
- http://www.airspacemag.com/military-aviation/flying-bombers-in-world-war-ii-1348897/: *Air & Space, Smithsonian – My Mother, The Bomber Pilot*
- http://www.boldmethod.com/blog/lists/2015/11/15-things-you-never-knew-about-the-b-17-flying-fortress/: *15 Things You Never Knew About The B-17 Flying Fortress (photos)*
- https://en.wikipedia.org/wiki/Nebraska_World_War_II_army_airfields : *Nebraska World War II army airfields were major United States Army Air Forces (USAAF) training centers for pilots and aircrews of USAAF fighters and bombers during World War II.*
- http://www.lincolnafb.org/history.php: *Lincoln Air Force Base: Second to None*

- https://en.wikipedia.org/wiki/South_Dakota_World_War_II_Army_Airfields: *During World War II, the United States Army Air Forces (USAAF) established numerous airfields in South Dakota for training pilots and aircrews of USAAF fighters and bombers.*
- https://eugenetoyandhobby.com/shop/revell-148-b-17g-flying-fortress/: *Photo of B-17*
- https://en.wikipedia.org/wiki/Norden_bombsight: *The Norden Mk. XV, known as the Norden M series in Army service, was a bombsight used by the United States Army Air Forces (USAAF) and the United States Navy during World War II . . .*
- https://masseyaero.org/news/Norden.html
- https://www.nps.gov/moru/index.htm: *Mount Rushmore*
- https://en.wikipedia.org/wiki/SS_%C3%8Ele_de_France: *SS Île de France (photo)*
- https://en.wikipedia.org/wiki/RMS_Queen_Mary: *With the outbreak of the Second World War, she was converted into a troopship and ferried Allied soldiers for the duration of the war.*
- http://RMSQueen Mary1Ship-HistoryandFacts (queenmarycruises.net) (photo)
- https://en.wikipedia.org/wiki/Boeing_B-17_Flying_Fortress: *The B-17 was primarily employed by the United States Army Air Forces (USAAF) in the daylight strategic bombing campaign of World War II against German industrial and military targets.*
- http://www.stelzriede.com/ms/html/mshwpmn1.htm: *B-17 Pilot Training Manual*
- http://www.controltowers.co.uk/8%20list%201.htm: *8th United Army Air Fields – UK Air Field Listing 1942-45*
- http://www.398th.org/Research/398th_FAQ.html: *FAQs about Army Air Force Terms in WWII*
- https://www.thebalance.com/aircraft-flight-instruments-the-basic-six-pack-282852: *6 Traditional Flight Instruments Pilots Need to Know*
- https://en.wikipedia.org/wiki/Bombardment_group: *A bombardment group or bomb group was a group of bomber aircraft the United States Army Air Forces (USAAF) during World War II.*

- https://en.wikipedia.org/wiki/Anti-aircraft_warfare: *Photo of German 88mm flak gun in action against Allied bombers.*
- https://en.wikipedia.org/wiki/Strategic_bombing_during_World_War_II: *Strategic bombing during World War II was the sustained aerial attack on railways, harbors, cities, workers' housing, and industrial districts in enemy territory . . .*
- https://www.whitehouse.gov/about-the-white-house/presidents/franklin-d-roosevelt/
- https://www.whitehouse.gov/about-the-white-house/presidents/harry-s-truman/
- https://www.americanairmuseum.com/media/4687 (Roger Freeman Collection): *Photo of B-17s lined up for take-off.*
- http://www.azquotes.com/author/1786-Omar_N_Bradley: *Omar N. Bradley Quotes – "The smell of death overwhelmed us even before we passed through the stockade"*
- https://www.dfcsociety.org/pages/the-distinguished-flying-cross-medal
- https://en.wikipedia.org/wiki/Distinguished_Flying_Cross_(United_States): *Additional history of the Distinguished Flying Cross (United States).*
- http://valor.militarytimes.com/list.php?category=Awards: *Hall of Valor – List of Recipients (with citations) who have received various medals for meritorious service or for combat actions.*
- https://en.wikipedia.org/wiki/Messerschmitt_Me_262: *History of the Messerschmitt Me 262*
- https://acepilots.com/german/me262_17.jpg: *Photo of a Messerschmitt Me 262*
- https://en.wikipedia.org/wiki/Focke-Wulf_Fw_190: *Photo of a Focke-Fw 190*
- https://www.ancestry.com/
- http://www.militaryfactory.com/aircraft/detail.asp?aircraft_id=108: *The German Messerschmitt Me 262 Schwalbe World War 2 became the first operational jet-powered fighter in military history.*
- http://www.americanwarlibrary.com/medlist.htm: *Lists of Military Medal Recipients*

- https://en.wikipedia.org/wiki/Brabag: *Brabag . . . while it operated, it produced commodities vital to the German military forces before and during World War II. After substantial damage from strategic bombing, the firm and its remaining assets were dissolved at the end of the war.*
- https://www.plasticstoday.com/business/design-world-war-ii-plastics-and-npe
- https://www.eia.gov/tools/faqs/faq.php?id=34&t=6#:~:text=Although%20crude%20oil%20is%20a,derived%20from%20crude%20oil%20refining
- https://en.wikipedia.org/wiki/Elie_Wiesel: *He was the author of 57 books, written mostly in French and English, including* Night, *a work based on his experiences as a prisoner in the Auschwitz and Büchenwald concentration camps.*
- http://www.pbs.org/auschwitz/maps/: *Auschwitz: Inside the Nazi State – Maps & Plans*
- https://en.wikipedia.org/wiki/Büchenwald_concentration_camp: *Büchenwald concentration camp was a German Nazi concentration camp established on Ettersberg hill near Weimar, Germany, in July 1937, one of the first and the largest of the concentration camps on German soil, following Dachau's opening just over four years earlier.*
- https://en.wikipedia.org/wiki/List_of_Nazi_concentration_camps
- https://en.wikipedia.org/wiki/Zeitz: *A bombing target of the Oil Campaign of World War II, the Brabag plant northeast of Zeitz . . .*
- https://en.wikipedia.org/wiki/Army_Air_Forces_Training_Command: *Army Air Forces Training Command was the initial organization to which new recruits were assigned upon entry into the Army Air Forces during World War II.*
- http://www.epperts.com/lfa/BB67.html: *Article: Buffalo Bayou – An Echo of Houston's Wilderness Beginnings (Grand Central Station) by Louis F. Aulbach*
- https://en.wikisource.org/wiki/Houston:_Where_Seventeen_Railroads_Meet_the_Sea: *The book contains an introduction section describing*

the city of Houston in Texas, and then follows with various illustrations and captions.

- http://www.aviation-history.com/north-american/p51.html: *The Aviation History Online Museum ~ P-51 Mustang*
- http://www.aviation-history.com/messerschmitt/bf109.html
- https://100thbg.com/index.php?option=com_content&view=article&id=247:lazzari-crew-history&catid=25:group-history&Itemid=581: *Laurence J. Lazzari Crew History*
- https://www.boeing.com/history/products/p-51-mustang.page: *A veteran of World War II and the Korean War, North American Aviation's P-51 Mustang was the first U.S. built fighter airplane to push its nose over Europe after the fall of France.*
- https://en.wikipedia.org/wiki/Messerschmitt_Bf_109: *The Messerschmitt Bf 109 is a German World War II fighter aircraft that was the backbone of the Luftwaffe's fighter force.*
- http://acepilots.com/german/me262_17.jpg: *Photo – ME-262*
- http://www.381st.org/Aircraft/B-17-Basics: *B-17 Bail Out photo.*
- http://www.in2guitar.com/b-17.html: *How to bail out of the B-17 Bomber.*
- http://forums.ubi.com/showthread.php/446009-Matching-Airspeed-across-altitudes-Forums/page2: *Photo of Combat Wing: Below and angled view.*
- https://www.britannica.com/biography/Adolf-Hitler/Dictator-1933-39: *Adolf Hitler*
- https://ww2db.com/battle_spec.php?battle_id=43: *Battle of Berlin*
- https://en.wikipedia.org/wiki/100th_Air_Refueling_Wing: *During World War II, its predecessor unit, the 100th Bombardment Group (Heavy), was an Eighth Air Force B-17 Flying Fortress unit in England, stationed at RAF Thorpe Abbotts.*
- https://en.wikipedia.org/wiki/Surrender_of_Japan: S*urrender of Imperial Japan announced on August 15 and formally signed on September 2, 1945, ending the hostilities of World War II.*
- https://en.wikipedia.org/wiki/Enola_Gay: *On 6 August 1945, during the final stages of World War II, it became the first aircraft to drop an atomic bomb.*

- https://www.atomicheritage.org/history/bombings-hiroshima-and-nagasaki-1945: *Atomic Heritage Foundation: Bombings of Hiroshima and Nagasaki – 1945.*
- https://en.wikipedia.org/wiki/Victory_in_Europe_Day: *The term VE Day existed as early as September 1944, in anticipation of victory.*
- https://en.wikipedia.org/wiki/Victory_over_Japan_Day: *V-J Day selected by Allies after they named V-E Day for victory in Europe.*
- http://www.strategic-air-command.com/bases/Goose_Bay_AFB.htm: *Map of Strategic Air Command Bases: Goose Bay Air Force Base*
- http://postalhistorycorner.blogspot.ca/2012/07/wwii-real-photo-postcards-german-pows.html: *WWII Real Photo Postcards German POWs Interned in Canada*
- https://en.wikipedia.org/wiki/Curtiss_C-46_Commando: *Used as military transport during WW II by the U.S. Army Air Forces . . .*
- https://www.afreserve.com/about: *Since President Harry S. Truman called for the formation of the Air Force Reserve in 1948, it has been a critical part of the nation's defense.*
- https://en.wikipedia.org/wiki/North_American_T-6_Texan: *The N.A. Aviation T-6 Texan is an American single-engine advanced trainer aircraft trained pilots of the U.S. Army Air Forces . . .*
- https://www.allaboutvision.com/contacts/faq/when-invented.htm: *When Were Contact Lenses Invented?*
- https://www.weather.gov/crp/hurricanecarla: *Hurricane Carla – 50th Anniversary*
- https://volcanoes.usgs.gov/volcanoes/st_helens/st_helens_geo_hist_99.html: *Mt. St. Helens – 1980 Cataclysmic Eruption*
- https://www.sciencealert.com/nearly-40-years-after-mount-st-helens-deadly-eruption-it-s-recharging: *Photo of Mt. St. Helens' Eruption*
- https://en.wikipedia.org/wiki/Thorpe_Abbotts: *During WWII, Thorpe Abbotts became home to an airbase with the designation 139, Thorpe Abbotts.*
- https://www.pinterest.com/annie1152/world-war-2/: *Photo: Briefing Room, 8th Air Force*

- http://www.benefits.va.gov/gibill/history.asp: *It has been heralded as one of the most significant pieces of legislation ever produced by the federal government . . .*
- https://www.nps.gov/thrb/learn/historyculture/tr-rr-spanamwar.htm: *Among Theodore Roosevelt's many lifetime accomplishments . . . a "Rough Rider" during the Spanish-American War.*
- https://www.oilandgas360.com/oil-the-30-year-anniversary-of-the-1986-collapse/: *It has been 30 years since the 1986 crude oil collapse . . .*
- http://www.cancer.net/navigating-cancer-care/side-effects/fluid-around-lungs-or-malignant-pleural-effusion
- https://www.thevintagenews.com/2016/05/05/top-10-hollywood-stars-served-wwii/: *Among the millions of Americans who answered the call to join the armed services . . . biggest names in film . . .*
- https://en.wikipedia.org/wiki/James_Stewart: *On July 23, 1959, Stewart was promoted to brigadier general.*
- https://www.airplaneboneyards.com/kingman-arizona-airplane-boneyard-storage.htm: *Photo: Aircraft parked and awaiting sale, or the furnaces, at Kingman AAF after World War II*
- https://pixels.com/featured/vintage-b-17-cockpit-mike-burgquist.html
- https://weather.com/storms/hurricane/news/tropical-storm-harvey-forecast-texas-louisiana-arkansas: *Catastrophic, Record Flooding in Southeast Texas*
- https://www.weather.gov/hgx/2021ValentineStorm

www.ingramcontent.com/pod-product-compliance
Lightning Source LLC
Chambersburg PA
CBHW051422090426
42737CB00014B/2795
9780999359556